The author, Brian Barber, lives in Stoke-on-Trent, where he has been involved in Christian youth work for many years. In that time he has been responsible for a remarkable youth group which has brought many young people into the life of the Church. This is the story of that group, together with advice and ideas on how to run a youth group wherever you are.

This Little Cloud

An Adventure in Christian Youth Work

Brian R. Barber

MOORLEY'S Print & Publishing

British Library Cataloguing in Publication Data.
A catalogue record for this book is available
from the British Library.

ISBN 0 86071 490 X

23 Park Rd., Ilkeston, Derbys DE7 5DA
Tel/Fax: (0115) 932 0643

in association with

12a Moorland Road, Burslem,
Stoke on Trent ST6 1DW

CONTENTS

DEDICATION

TO MUM AND DAD

without whose love, support and guidance
none of this would have been possible.

FOREWORD

by

Rev. Dr. Rob Frost

Of all the youth groups I have ever visited, I would put the 'Group' in the Potteries as the most imaginative, fruitful and effective. This is the story of this remarkable group, told simply and with frankness. It will give strength to many youth leaders who feel like giving up, and the section of advice and ideas will stimulate others to make a new start.

Lots of books about youth work are written by experts who've never done effective youth work themselves. Not so with this book. Whenever anyone asks me for advice on youth groups I refer them to Brian. He's not a theory man, he gets the job done.

PREFACE

Tunstall was the centre of the Primitive Methodist revival of the nineteenth century. As Potteries people will know, every great event deserves to be celebrated in clay, and I have in my possession one of the plates thrown to commemorate the Primitive Methodist centenary of 1907. Over pictures of Hugh Bourne and William Clowes and their first chapels are the words "The little cloud's increasing still which first arose upon Mow Hill." This book is one of those little clouds, maybe a sign of the times, maybe only a passing shower. But it is not written in any sense to glorify the work of a person or a group of people. God has given us each our talents, but unless they are infused by His presence they cannot be fully used for Him. All that follows here is His work, and is only one very faint thread in the large embroidered tapestry of Christian history. But the book is written because I want to say something about Christian Youth work in this country in the last part of the twentieth century. "Christ is not dead, He is alive," the old chorus goes. If we proclaim that to our young people, if we can only learn to communicate it in terms they can understand, then I am convinced their response now will be as real and as revolutionary as it has ever been. And whether we be minister, youth leader or pew pusher, to lead another to Christ and help him or her through those early exciting stages of Christian growth is to know real fulfilment. Let us speak to this barren wilderness which is England from our oasis of Christian experience, that the thirsty may drink, and with new strength turn the world upside down like the young apostles of old.

May I thank those friends who reminded me of events I had partly forgotten, and corrected my mistakes, and particularly Mrs. Rosemary Nixon and Mary Adams who gave their time to type the original manuscript. The first edition appeared locally in 1976. This edition is extensively revised and updated. My thanks to Sue Ball, who typed it.

Brian R. Barber.
Revised edition: March 1997

Chapter 1

ADD A LAD

"The conversion of an adult is the addition of a unit, the conversion of a lad is the addition of a multiplication table to the Church of Christ." When I found those words again after a break of many years, their reality in my own experience was very humbling. I read the letter through carefully: "Your grand story of answered prayer in the conversion of that one who knelt at the communion rail reminded me of the story of the Scottish elder who after a mission, said, 'Only one convert, and that was only a boy – wee Bobbie Moffat. And 'wee Bobbie Moffat' led David Livingstone to go to Africa, and David Livingstone – led??? Mr. Chadwick said, as perhaps you remember, "The conversion of an adult is the addition of a unit, the conversion of a lad is the addition of a multiplication table to the Church of Christ. Who knows what your answered prayer may mean in the years to come". This letter was slipped through my letter box a few days after my own conversion. It was written by Rev. George Allen, at 83 a cripple by arthritis, but a Christian sure of his faith, in response to a letter written to him by an elderly lady in my home congregation, Mrs. Beresford, asking him to explain to her the strange circumstances of my own conversion to Christ.

Although I had been brought up in a Methodist Sunday School, I had reached that period of adolescence when such activities seemed childish, and I had left. Not before chapel-going had got under my skin however. And although I did not know what I believed, the Methodist community seemed a sort of home. I went irregularly to Church on a Sunday morning, and joined, more or less, enthusiastically in the youth activities of my local chapel.

In the Easter holidays of my last year at school, the third large Methodist Chapel in Tunstall, King Street, organised a 'Mission', a two week visitation by four ministerial students in training, and two deaconesses, in another of several fairly regular attempts to present the gospel to the people of Tunstall.

Some friends easily persuaded me to attend the first night of the Mission, which was held in King Street Sunday School Hall, a large bare brick, wooden-floor boarded room under the Church. I don't remember now much about the meeting; I suppose it was typical of such events, with hymn and testimony and message punched home. But I do remember that at its close, the speaker asked all those who wished to commit their lives to Christ to stand up, and as, one after the other, they rose, I became more and more convinced of their "hypocrisy" – "they're only following their friends", I told myself; "they don't know what they're doing – what a farce the whole thing is!" And I determined not to come to the mission again. Nevertheless, something must have been sparked off in my mind, because for the next ten days I struggled with doubts. Did I believe in God? Was there a purpose behind the Universe? Who was Jesus Christ? Did He rise from the dead? And was God alive there and then, and could he do anything for me?

By Easter Sunday, the last day of the campaign, the only thing that I had resolved was that this uncertainty had depressed me, and when urged to attend the final rally, I was an easy sell. I have been told since that the Mission had not gone well. The weather was very poor; visiting and outdoor speaking had been seriously interfered with; and the response had been far from enthusiastic. But there had been prayer - particular individuals were prayed for, and much was hoped for the final evening.

What I remember most clearly is that part way through the service I came to faith and commitment. There was a brass vase of daffodils on the left of the big central dark stained pulpit. I was sitting three rows from the front, and as the preacher waded into his message, my mind wandered to those flowers. So beautiful, so delicate, made with such loving care! The Creator was responsible, and His love for the flowers was an expression of His love for mankind which extended even to me. God loved me, and He had shown that love in His Son whose resurrection we were that day celebrating. They were a symbol of the new life which could be mine. What could I do other than offer my love in return? In the first line of the first verse of the last hymn I pushed my way past my brother and a whole line of young people to kneel at the Communion rail and commit my life to Christ. It was just like light breaking in.

No-one else responded, and I was amazed to be told by friends, after I came out of the counselling room, that they had been praying for me. I didn't know anyone else was the slightest concerned!

A few days later that letter arrived through the post. Mrs. Beresford's son was named Brian, and, as I was the only Brian in the congregation that night, she had been praying for me. I can't pretend that there was an overnight dramatic change. It was inside that I felt different. A sense of God's presence, and a reliance on Him gave me purpose and peace, but left me with many problems to solve.

But I write knowing that, had that challenge not been presented to me, I would probably not today be more than an occasional chapel-goer with a rather vague, uninformed belief in a God beyond; I would not have followed my career as a teacher; I would not be a preacher of the gospel; and I would not have found the relationships and experiences which have enriched my life ever since.

It is for that reason that I have come to believe that challenge is at the heart of the Christian gospel - a challenge to discipleship, to adventure, to surrender - a challenge which it is the duty of the Church to present at every available opportunity so that we might by all means win some. As I read the New Testament, it seems clear to me that Jesus Christ accepted that challenge Himself when He went to the cross. With humanity and divinity inextricably intertwined, the love of God burst through in the life of a man, so that when the human form was broken and shattered, the divine spirit could still call down God's forgiveness. And on many occasions He called men to follow, to give up all right to themselves, to save their lives by losing them for His sake and the gospel's. How strange those words of command must have seemed ringing through the still air over the sea of Galilee, plain and powerful in the streets of the busy towns, hushed yet urgent in the balmy night air. Men did not always follow; some had their businesses to build up, others felt the pressures of materialism; some looked for proof in signs, others rationalised their narrow minded view of life. And somehow the breadth and the vision of the gospel passed them by; they were the grey characters whose very souls seem choked in the sad dust of death. Glorious technicolour was reserved for Peter, the impetuous fisherman who learned what it was to be a loving fisher of men, Mary of Magdala whose capacity for love was used in the service of her Lord, Thomas the doubter who discovered the faith of an obedient heart. And where the history of the Church down the centuries glows with the same radiance, it is where the individual man or woman has discovered that superhuman commitment whose activities seem infused with the very spirit of God; Augustine and Aquinas, Luther and Cranmer, Wesley, Booth, Mother Theresa and Martin Luther King, those famous and those who now have no name, but whose names their Lord knows.

It has always been that moment of 'turning round', that first response to the call of God, that sense of personal inadequacy, and acceptance of the indwelling life of Christ, that has been the driving force of their lives.

It's a great game to play – to search the records of the pages of history for those holy moments when the saints of God first found faith. And in our grey world, when sadness and drabness lick their dry and dusty lips over the prospect of lost and broken lives, the call of Jesus seems to ring just as clear: "Unless a man be born again, he cannot enter the Kingdom of God." Babies are born in very different circumstances and stages of growth, but until they are born, they are not born! I often think that this was the important part of Christ's analogy. It is in the belief that this new birth, this commitment, surrender or dedication, this conversion, repentance or acceptance, or whatever label you may wish to tag, is the intended way by which it becomes possible to enter the fulfilment of the Christian life, that I write this book. The events which follow add their small voice to the drowning crescendo of Christian witness.

Chapter 2

IN THE BEGINNING

I have come to believe that a continuous series of 'coincidences' are an unlikely coincidence in total. Much more likely in the life of the Christian is the direction and guidance of God. To look back over the Christian years is to see the binding ties of an almost invisible silver chord tying events together in a marvellous way which previously seemed unconnected. By a series of such 'coincidences' I spent most of my time at University living in the very College whose students had led the Tunstall Mission. Hartley Victoria College, Manchester, was a training ground for prospective Methodist Ministers. Standing almost opposite Alexandra Park, and a building full of rambling dark corridors in those days, it laid claim to be the largest Protestant theological College in Europe. The matron could quote exactly how many 'miles' of linoleum there were, and the students spoke proudly of its Primitive Methodist evangelical traditions. Hugh Bourne's boot was under a show case in the library; a picture of Mow Cop, the scene of those early camp meetings, glowered down at the library tables, and the noseless statue of William Hartley, the jam benefactor, added to the sense of history – he had lost his nose when lying in a bed in which he had been placed during inter-college scenes of rivalry with another theological College! It was a lively place; I quickly came to realise that ministers were just ordinary men, called by God to a particular life of service. Their holiness was for the most part practical and down to earth, and supported by a real sense of humour. It was here that I learned my first faltering steps in the Christian life, and Chapel prayers and the fellowship of 'tea club' enabled me to sort out my views and problems. I owe the place an unpayable debt, and I, at least, will always be grateful to God for the tutors and students of that era who helped me to see the relevance of Christ to every part of life. Although its building is sadly now not used as a theological College, I often in my memory sit in the Common Room and pray in the Chapel, and I know its spirit infuses my bones.

And that spirit is the spirit of evangelism. I had not been reared in such traditions; the enthusiasm of the 'Ranters' had long been lost in Tunstall, and I was really to stumble by accident upon the power of the preacher's plain call to commitment. But everything I learned seemed to reinforce the growing idea that the Church had lost its way because it no longer made Christ's call to discipleship its first priority.

I studied Law and Theology at Manchester University, and during this time sought my vocation. After much consideration, learning and prayer, I decided to train to be a teacher of Religious Education, and spent a year at Didsbury College of Higher Education for my Teacher's

Certificate. The result of a range of applications for teaching posts brought me back again to my home City.

My first teaching appointment was in a boys' technical grammar school, Stanfield, where I was to teach Religious Studies and English. Here I was to learn how to build relationships with young people and to teach Religious Studies in as objective, academic and factual way as I could.

The question of 'brainwashing' by R.E. Teachers at secondary level, is, I submit, largely an irrelevant controversy. If the Church, through its Christian teachers, has been engaged in brainwashing techniques over the years, its methods have been very inept, for the decline in Church attendance and belief has rarely in the history of the Church in this country been more marked than in the twentieth century. Of course we are all involved in, and have been subjected to, indoctrination in every field of human endeavour. It is the stuff of which civilisation is made. The social and moral training of the home, the attitudes and prejudices, of society, the tendency towards materialism with its emphasis on what you earn rather than how you earn it, are part and parcel of the development of the growing child. And I submit that no one, parent, teacher, employer, can opt out of the educational process, or act as a 'neutral chairman' in his relationship with any other, because just by being himself, by speaking, behaving, reacting, by his very existence, he is a formative influence on all those who come into contact with him. "No man is an island entire of itself." John Donne said it well long years ago; we are part of one another, "So send not to know for whom the bell tolls; it tolls for thee". But in the field of faith, such 'indoctrination' has no real effect unless the individual consciously and willingly appropriates the faith he is taught to himself. He does not have faith unless it is his own faith; a learned second-hand set of beliefs are not what the Bible understands by being in Christ. The job of the Christian teacher is more to educate the child or young person so that he may have sufficient knowledge and understanding to be able to make an informed decision for or against faith. Ignorance is the enemy of the educator, and ignorance is bliss as far as religion and the English family are concerned. In those early years of my teaching career when it was still accepted that Christianity was almost the whole of the religious education syllabus, I quickly found that children arriving at Stanfield did not know the Old from the New Testament, could not separate John the Baptist from Joshua, and had largely rejected their own childish and incomplete view of God, rather than God himself. I saw it as my job to fill in the gaps in their knowledge, and help them to understand this Jesus and His Gospel for themselves. Even today I do not believe it is possible or desirable for the R.E. teacher to be in the role of a neutral chairman. A religious stance shows itself best in actions rather than words, and developing young people want to know the stance of the various adults in their little world, so that they can use it as a buffer against which they formulate their own views. "Some scholars think" is usually followed by the question, "But what do you think sir?" – in fact it became a joke among the sixth formers I taught that every time I used that first phrase that it was possible that I was using it as a guise for my own views. They were mistaken to assume that, but, in any case, those views were not automatically accepted; they splashed into the pool of ideas, to be stirred around vigorously. But at least they would get a hearing, which is far from true in many areas of the country in these present days of religious, moral and social decline.

Relationships are the essence of teaching. I made the young teacher's familiar disastrous mistake – if I'm gentle with them, they will respond in kind. So my first year was spent in battening down the hatches to hold down the flood waters of indiscipline, and learning how firmness and authority do not debar friendship and understanding.

I felt God had called me to work among young people, and I wanted to express this through service to the Church. So I began a Youth Club at Wesley Place Methodist Church in Tunstall, and I was volunteered to teach in the Young People's Department of the Sunday School there. The Church had really declined during my years away – each time I came home, the congregation seemed smaller and more depressed. There were no other young people my age, and only about three people under 40 in the normal evening congregation. I thought a Youth Club would be a useful outreach to the community and I obtained the permission of the Church leaders meeting to use the main Sunday School Hall for table tennis, billiards, records and coffee on a Thursday evening weekly. It was a most disillusioning experience. About thirty young people gathered regularly, a few from the Sunday School, but they were mostly unchurched. My programme of activities and discussions met with little support; the most attractive feature of the Club as far as the members were concerned was the annual outing to Blackpool, calling at various pubs on the way; and although the rather rough breed of youngster we drew in was reasonably polite, he was more successful at unchurching the churched than vice versa.

A few weeks after taking over my Sunday School class, I was left with two girls to teach on most Sundays, Kay and Kathleen. It irked me that as I was teaching these two on a Sunday afternoon, across Tunstall square, at Jubilee Chapel, another teacher was doing the same with another smallish group of teenagers, and in the end I decided to take Church unity into my own hands by taking my class to join his. This proved to be a forerunner of the uniting of the two Sunday Schools, for the monolithic Methodist empires in Tunstall whose origins lay in Primitive and Wesleyan Methodism were even then creaking and groaning their way towards a unity dictated by economics and common sense. Eventually Jubilee Sunday School were to desert their premises, lecture hall and all, and use the Sunday School rooms, renamed the Youth Centre, at Wesley Place, while the Wesley Place Chapel was to close and its congregation unite in worship at Jubilee Chapel.

Very shortly after the two groups of young people came together, I was given charge of their class. Christian commitment for these young people became my undeclared aim, and discussion seemed the most likely way of achieving it. Discussion means involvement. It is so easy within the traditional patterns of organisation of Church and Sunday School for the participant to remain totally non-involved, to switch his mind off and go through the religious mumbo-jumbo without ever considering in depth its relevance for him. To listen to a speaker, however brilliant, is to be as passive as the present national T.V. audience, unless he requires response, and T.V. has so impinged our national consciousness today that we sit and listen to the weekly preacher with the thought, "Come on, entertain me!" If he is boring, no matter how worthy, then he is a flop. And when he has finished, no matter how he has spoken to the total me, I can switch off the set of the mind, and turn my attention elsewhere. But to participate in discussion is to spin the cogs of the brain, and to speak is to be totally involved. I can listen to the point of view of other real people who sit as near to me as breathing, and the conflict of ideas begins to stir my inner thoughts. Where do I stand? What do I think?

Discussion in this young people's class was not easy; few of them had confidence either in themselves, in me or in their knowledge of the gospel, but we plodded our way through awkward pauses and bored politeness towards a slightly more satisfactory questioning period. The trouble was, the situation seemed so false. Here we were sitting in upright chairs in a circle round a brown wooden desk in a bare church vestry on a Sunday afternoon, snatched from our homes, the Sunday roast and the telly to do our 'religious' bit before we dropped back again into our normal relationships and our everyday lives. It was the House Group era, and I was led to propose at a Church leaders' meeting that our Church begin one such, rather more natural, informal meeting in someone's home. This was accepted, and Eric Brereton, the Superintendent of the Sunday School and I, were placed in charge of it. We decided together that this should be for young people, and should meet on a Sunday evening fortnightly. We combed the Church for teenagers, and offered a warm encouraging invitation to our first evening discussion together. They came rather nervously, but they came, and that was what mattered. A rather mundane set of events: two Churches struggling to find new life, a young man doing his best to express his commitment as realistically as he could; nothing particularly remarkable here. And yet this whole series of events leading to that decision to start a young peoples' house group were to be the catalyst out of which God's activity grew in a very startling and dramatic way.

Chapter 3
ALL THINGS WORK TOGETHER

We were a small, if motley band, who assembled at a church member's house on that first Sunday evening, four or five teenagers, the Superintendent, myself. The atmosphere was frozen – this was after all a pioneering venture, and such ventures interfere with people's security. We discussed, and then we fed well. The discussion as I remember it was about our role in the Church. What did we think of the services? What ought the Church to be doing? How could we be involved in it? We sat warm and comfortable in deep armchairs sharing an occasional rather stilted thought, and after about an hour of meandering discourse, were treated to a palatial supper by our hosts. Food in fact became a feature of those early meetings. Parents of the members laid on buffet suppers in their own homes, so lavish a meal often that Sunday tea had to disappear, and the events took on the nature of a social occasion. We only discussed once a month; on the other occasion we played table games or listened to music or chatted together. And we began to build up real friendships, so strong that members came to feel themselves threatened by any new arrival. I went to Church every Sunday evening, and took to sitting in the same place. Without ever mentioning the need to attend, but by talking about what took place there, I eventually encouraged a full pew of teenagers to attend.

Jubilee, where we worshipped, was a huge and very beautiful chapel. It was a gallery church built to house the Primitive Methodist Conferences of the late nineteenth and early twentieth centuries. It held 1,200 and was dominated by a high central pulpit of light oak where the preacher could swing several cats if he wished. The congregation filled about a tenth of the available seats. We sat on the back row in the gallery miles away from the preacher - binoculars and hearing aids would not have been out of place! The young people were largely attentive – it must have seemed a strange occupation for them to be in the midst of those decent, well – dressed orderly chapel folk, going through the routine of the invariable hymn sandwich, when they were more used to 'Top of the Pops' or the atmosphere of the Boothen End at Stoke City Football Ground.

Our discussions were tough going. I had decided to begin with a book called "The Daily Life of the Christian" by John Murray, which examined those social questions which particularly concerned the believer. I gave a five minute chapter summary, and plunged into a set of prepared questions, using all the techniques of the discussion groups of the University Methodist Society where I had been President for a year. I quickly discovered that these were inadequate for a different audience, not so ready to participate, and uninformed about even the most obvious matters. In fact, my techniques were learned by stumbling error rather than any other way.

I could, for example, answer my own questions, and talk almost continuously to pass the time, or I could ask loaded questions that implied the 'correct' answer, or drew the brief and stunning 'yes' or 'no'. I came to see that painful silences were embarrassing in the short run, but long term enabled people to find their tongues, if only to save their red faces. And open ended discussions were useless for this age group. I had to know where I was going if they were to learn anything. To have in my mind the fact that only a spiritual experience of Christ would make Christian behaviour meaningful meant that every road led back to Him, even though the young people often walked the road blindfold. The only person beside myself who had a real understanding of Christianity was Christine Rowe, a young middle school teacher active in the Sunday School. We very soon lost several members, but of those who remained, Melvyn, John, and Keith were High School boys, the last named attending the school where I taught. Keith's girl-friend at that time was Gill, a grammar school girl. Of this group, only John was really talkative; the others were often very shy, and at that stage rather wrapped up in themselves. With Kath, these were to be the 'stickers' among the original group, even though their stickability was at times rather shaky.

In September 1967, the Church was to receive a new minister. I had prayed quite fiercely that it might be a man who was sympathetic to positive evangelism, and had been encouraged when I managed to arrange a ' chance ' meeting with him before he arrived officially. The caretaker told me that he was to visit the church, so I was 'absent-mindedly' moving some books when he came in, and we had a very short conversation. Claud Thompson – short, white haired, dark glasses, piercing eyes and an accent I did not recognise – that was my initial impression, coupled with an immediate awareness of his spiritual concern. On his first Sunday evening, he preached on "Christ for all; all for Christ" and I knew I had found a friend. I was a frequent visitor to his house, and quickly came to share the ups and downs of the personnel of the House Group with both him and his wife. One of his sons, David was living at home, and became a lively and good humoured member of the group, able to offer a Christian lead in a rather more light hearted way than I was myself.

The other important event of those early days was a Circuit Youth Conference. I had been elected Circuit Youth Secretary, and met the various young people and keen youth leaders associated with other churches in the circuit. Among these was Marilyn, a young secondary school teacher, who was to play a large part in the development of the Tunstall Youth Group. The Circuit had long had a policy of bringing the young people of its Churches together in weekend and day conferences, and every effort was made to revive these, including a day out at the Cheshire Cat restaurant, Nantwich, when Arthur Shaw the Chairman of the District talked on the personality of Jesus. The descriptions were brilliant, the Bible leapt to life, and I remember learning many new insights on the many sided facets of Christ's character. But the young people were not used to listening, and the Biblical material was new and strange to them. They remember better today the restaurant meals, though I have little doubt that some of the Chairman's enthusiasm and knowledge rubbed off. Our Methodist 'Bishop' remained a keen supporter and encourager, and grew to be loved by the people of the Youth Group in the years to come. Nevertheless, what happened that day was only a small step on our journey. Of more significance was the Sunday Conference we arranged at Keele University for April 21st, 1968. Although I was myself to be away on holiday, I was involved in the arrangements for a small conference where everything seemed to go wrong until everything suddenly went right. The Conference was based on the experience of Christians in the twentieth century. We showed a film about the experience of the Bishop of Birmingham as a prisoner of war in Japan, and we persuaded Celia Prophett to come and speak. She was a young woman who had a very promising career until she was struck with sclerosis in the middle of her University course, leaving her almost blind. She turned this tragedy into a triumph by her determined Christian faith, and became actively involved as a teacher, youth leader and local preacher. We knew her story would speak to the heart. Getting good numbers, getting people there and providing them with food each had its own difficulty, but the major disaster was that there was no sound from the film, and the group watched Japanese scenes of torture and the shining faith of a clergyman in eerie silence. The Bishop had been tortured as a Japanese prisoner-of-war, and wondered how he could live out the Christian ethic of love towards those very men who were, so cruelly and fiendishly, trying to destroy his faith. He felt he had failed to communicate the love of Christ, but after the war he administered Communion to one of his torturers who had been converted by what he saw of the Bishop's faith.

The final service of the Conference was held in Keele Chapel, which is an ecumenical worship centre, with its own small chapel for the free churches. The small group of twenty seemed to be spiritually uplifted in this setting, and Marilyn felt moved to appeal for decisions for Christ. A small group from Red Street Church responded, as did Melvyn, and a lad from our own Sunday School, Alan. It was the first time we had seen any response to our efforts, and we were really glad. But young Christians need help, and Marilyn and I decided that we must give them opportunity of fellowship together, so we wrote notes to each one who had made a decision inviting them to a meeting at Marilyn's on Wednesday, May 1st, So what became known as 'Mal's Meet' had its beginnings.

The end of the Easter term had provided me with an opportunity to produce some religious drama at school. A short play called "We want Barabbas" had been written by David Lavis and a group of Methsoc students including myself when we had been on campaign in Keighley some years earlier. The play was published, and I arranged to perform it both at school and at church, with a group of school students, including Paul, Cliff, Trevor and Rob. The play imagines Barabbas to have returned to the scene of the crucifixion and to have been converted by the suffering love of Christ. It requires voices sitting in the audience chanting as though they were the Good Friday crowd, and a cross and crown of thorns to represent the crucifixion. The boys were very helpful; most of them had little or no connection with any church, but they willingly came down on a Sunday afternoon to help me black out the windows. Tall, stained glass, metal framed, windows with sloping window sills do not take kindly to drawing pins and blue drapes, and hours of struggling and laughter brought us closer together. It was good to be able to break down the barriers which formed the natural relationships between staff and students at school, and to be able to talk about the meaning behind the play. The Church congregation received it silently and respectfully, but it was different in front of the assembled school on the last afternoon of term. The empty cross with a light shining on it (instead of from behind) and the holly leaf crown stretched adolescent's imaginations too far and their reaction was laughter and noise in a darkened hall. It was hard for the actors but they bravely stuck to their posts. I was shattered by the effort of it all, and the rather disappointing reaction. I didn't then know what a foundation it had laid.

So House Group, Circuit Youth Conferences and school drama were the disparate elements which acted as the catalyst from which committed young lives would spring. I took some fifth formers to Swanwick for the National Fifth Formers Conference in July that year. The Christian Education Movement had made elaborate preparations to enable the fifth formers to express the theme of the Conference in the use of art, music, drama, poetry, audio- visual aids, discussion, interview and so on. The place was a hive of activity. Fifth formers off their reins tend to run riot, so it was good that there was plenty to do. The gospel crept in by implication, as was that body's style, but some antennae were quivering, just the same. My own group were a mixed bunch. Some were out to have a good time, but others were caught and affected by the challenge to idealism which the speakers hammered home. They were sad to leave. I dropped them off at their homes on by one, until only Trevor was left in the car. He showed me a picture he had painted during the Conference - dark edged, with a red glowing centre, and a circular crown of thorns whose white points seemed to reach out into the outer extremities of the picture, and he explained the darkness of the world into which the suffering love of Jesus reached. We sat and chatted for a long time; he had no church background, but he had been reached by the claims of Jesus, and when he got out of the car, I somehow felt that this conversation was a symbol of hope for the future.

Chapter 4

BY YON BONNIE BANKS

We had begun to grow so close together that it seemed right for the House Group to join one another on holiday. We settled on Scotland as the venue, and arranged to be away for the last two weeks in August. Kathleen, Christine, Melvyn, Keith, David, Gill and I were all keen to go, and we invited Mal to accompany us. Gill had a good friend who lived some way out of the city, a girl named Sandy, and she was interested too. Keith and Melvyn had half arranged to spend the summer at Butlins with two lads from Stanfield. But the idea of taking a mini-bus, and camping on western shores proved far more attractive, and provided the first outreach opportunity for the group. "Would you like to go to Scotland in a mini-bus? Come to our group on Sunday night then." So the two lads were caught up in the spirit of a possible adventure.

Will, a small curly haired boy, came first, to be followed shortly after by Melvyn No.2. The small group of friends had grown close enough to be a clique, and some of them did not appreciate intruders. Melvyn was very quiet, and when it came to lifts home on a Sunday night, he would often get left out. He sensed a certain resentment to his presence, which was not completely wrong; this increased his feelings of shyness, and at the end of almost every Monday afternoon R.E. lesson with the fifth form he would tell me how much he hated the group, and how he had no intention of coming on holiday with us. But somehow I always managed to talk him round, and there were eleven of us still when we left the Potteries on August 16th. None of us were experienced in camping, and, rather than land in the soup, (purely metaphorical!) we had loaded up the mini-bus with everything short of the kitchen sink, including a huge packet of 'Swel' potatoes of which we used only a couple of table-spoons worth at one meal, and almost as large a packet of custard powder. The two tents we had borrowed from the scouts were in average condition; usually we had to wedge the centre pole of one of them with a table tennis bat, and a combination of separate ground sheet and very wet weather taught us much about the delights of camping!

But we were always in good spirits, and experiences fair and foul brought us together in a way which few other events could have done. When we arrived in Oban it was raining heavens hard; we watched other campers baling out and vowed we would not put up our tents that night. We paddled, soaked, through the deserted streets until we saw a Scottish Presbyterian Church notice board with the name and address of the local minister on it, and an idea was born. I knocked on the door of the manse, dressed in a long packamack and soggy jeans, and announced I had a youth group who could not camp, and could we please borrow the church hall for the night. We were whisked into a warm study with fitted carpet, fed on cheese on toast, and all arrangements were made. The minister rang his sidesman for the key, and while we sat and munched and chatted, the heating was put on; we were glad to welcome the warm, dry, spacious, bare premises, and turn vestries into bedrooms with our camp beds. There was hot water in the kitchen, a room for a meeting place, and luxury of luxuries – two toilets! We were in these premises for three nights, and when we left a donation behind, I blessed the minister and his wife who had taught my friends a profound lesson about the caring ministry of the Church.

At Balmacara, we camped in a field which was an official camp-site, and could not decide which was worst – the overpowering smell of the drains, nearly sinking in the mud, or being continually drenched in the driving rain. The boys spent most of their time locked in the mini-bus playing cards, much to the annoyance of everyone else. A visit to Skye was just as rain washed, and we spent our hours there drying out in the Kings Head Hotel lounge in front of a roaring fire.

We crossed by the Strome ferry on our way to Kinlochewe, and by one of those miracles of coincidence took the wrong way through the village of Shieldaig, twenty houses and two shops, on the shore of Loch Torridon. The sun broke through, and, on a green overlooking the loch, we camped and dried out. It is a beautiful spot; typical Scotland - serene and peaceful, surrounded by mountains, and the loch blue and still. The stars at night were big and bright - we lay a long time gazing at them, meditating on eternity and infinity - and during the day the warm sunny weather meant sun and loch bathing. Our only problem was the gnats. Meals were eaten either locked in the mini-bus, or walking round in circles as fast as possible, and when Will lay out of the tent one night, he woke up with his eyes almost closed by gnat bites. The nearest church was the free Presbyterian Church, the "wee frees" as they are known. At midday on Sunday we attended the service in blissful ignorance of their different style of living. We were in jeans; the congregation was in dark suits and bucket bonnets. The man at the door seemed rather surprised at the invading hordes, but we filed into the plain simple church and sat in two rows near the back on the left hand side. What followed was an experience in worship never to be forgotten. With no organ, the singing, from what we thought at first was a Gaelic hymn book, but which turned out to be a book of very long Scottish 'psalms', was begun by a precentor - and the congregation sang what sounded to us like a series of low and high moans at funeral pace. We stood for the long prayer, and listened to a sermon of 55 minutes about the eternal dangers of desecrating the Sabbath, while the congregation consumed several pounds of sweets, and propped themselves up on the hymn rest, eyes glazed and staring. Doubtless the worship was very real for the Scottish worshippers, but it was a real culture shock to us. To control laughter, my own as well as theirs, proved almost impossible, and the event became a real group fisherman's tale as the years passed.

We left for Pitlochry, and as the magical charm of Shieldaig lifted, our holiday nearly ended in disaster. A tyre burst on the mini-bus when we were coming down a narrow one track road, with a ditch to the left and a steep mountainous drop to the right. The bus swayed from right to left dangerously, but eventually ended on its side in the ditch, the left front panel badly crumpled. The large packet of custard powder burst open, covering the windows, and running out through the back door to leave a trail of yellow down the road (it was raining again!). The bus stopped dead, there was a long silence, and then I enquired "Is everyone all right?" An affirmative answer, and we climbed out shakily. When the bus was towed from the ditch, and tyre changed, it proved driveable, and we were able to continue on our way. Nothing like an accident to make you aware of your responsibilities! Our last two nights were spent in bed and breakfast places in Edinburgh, in time for the Edinburgh Festival and the Tattoo, and the benefits of comfort and civilisation.

It was a holiday to remember, and it cemented relationships successfully. Melvyn wrote to his mother in the following terms, "I was wrong about the holiday. These are great people, and I'm having a wonderful time. Wish you were here."

Chapter 5
THE BREAKTHROUGH

The post-holiday sessions sprang to life. Will and Melvyn No.2, were firmly anchored members of the House Group, and suddenly, almost from nowhere, our membership increased. Trevor joined us, after an abortive attempt at Sunday school teaching elsewhere; Phil, a member of the Red Street Church, and a miner's son, attracted by the work of the Youth Council, joined the ranks. He had been held in the Church only by being given the job of pumping the organ for the Sunday service; he had no real conception of Christianity, and as a working teenager with money, made the most of the entertainment offerings of modern Britain, dancing, drinking and football. Lively and good humoured, he had not been able to make the most of the educational opportunities he had. Ann joined because she and her parents had made a New Year's resolution to attend Church regularly, and our new outreach meant she was quickly snapped up. Pauline joined us, as did Sylvia, a Wesley Place girl home from teacher training in Manchester. Our numbers had suddenly become too big for a front room, and we moved home to Wesley Place Sunday School premises. Jubilee was now being used as the Church, and Wesley Place Sunday School had become the Youth Department, and a range of activities took place there, including a Monday night Badminton club, a good recruiting centre. We were in a down-town area; the waste lands around made the Youth Centre look like the only building miraculously to survive a nuclear explosion. The Civic authorities were pulling down the rows of blackened terraced houses, to rebuild the whole of the 'top' end of Tunstall The Churches were under C.P.O. and deterioration set in fast. You entered the Youth Centre through a series of double doors and porches. To your left stretched a long, brown, red-tiled corridor leading to the now closed Church, with tiny vestries leading off, cluttered with rubbish, jumble and the remains of last year's Christmas fair. Ahead was a large hall with a narrow stage; high roofed, floorboarded, cold and draughty, with another set of vestries at the far end, and a kitchen to the left. Below it was a lesser hall, and beyond that two smaller rooms for primary and beginners' Sunday School classes. The premises were not at all attractive in their decor - in fact, during the time we used them, they were old fashioned and depressing. We were to discover that it was their atmosphere which attracted. It became a matter of constant amazement that young people ten miles or more away would spend their hard earned money every Sunday night to travel to such a place. We purloined one of the bottom smaller rooms next to the lesser hall. We hung curtains, and members of the congregation gave us armchairs they no longer needed. There was an old carpet and a coal fire, and a feeling of home. Here we gathered, twenty of us now, every Sunday night throughout 1969, with the same lavish buffets brought from members' homes, but with discussions every week at the request of the young people. I took the "Partners in Learning" series as my guide.

In December that year the Circuit organised a Youth Conference in Coventry. John F. Kennedy House was the Youth Centre attached to Coventry Cathedral, built in the same modern style, and often staffed by foreign volunteers, whose cheerful cooking did not always agree with the English palate. The Friday night offering of plastic garlic on toast did not quench our spirits. Pete Lewis a Christian gospel singer and guitarist, brought life to the company; I had persuaded some of the young people to attend, including Trevor, who successfully ducked out of certain significant sessions to explore the delights of Coventry. Anyone with an artistic sense cannot fail to thrill to the magnificent symbolism of the Cathedral; to walk from its old bombed out ruins on a cold December morning into the light and colour of modern man's worship of God is a spiritual experience in itself. On Sunday morning, Trevor went to communion in the Cathedral by himself, and in receiving bread and wine for the first time, consciously and quietly received into himself the life of Christ. But we were not to know for some time.

March saw Melvyn No.2's membership service; his was a quiet, solid, practical witness, never dramatic, always controlled. But the Youth Group members were there, and heard him vow his love of Christ, a service to be repeated so many times as individuals came to Christ, that the congregation were heard to ask why these young people could not all become members together! In fact the early contacts between Church and young people were often difficult. The members of Mal's Meet and the members of the Youth Group wanted something positive to do, and one of the suggestions made was that they should lead worship. Mal's Meet became a 'Mission Band' and the Group took the occasional Youth Service, whose non-traditional approach often resulted in a disastrous response. We performed an Easter extract from "A Man Born to be King" by Dorothy L. Sayers by broadcasting it from the Church vestry into a darkened Church on April 6th, and this proved to be one of our more successful ventures.

As the new members became more integrated, so opposition to my leadership grew. I was emphasising the spiritual, many of them wanted something more social. It was the Club versus Group controversy. Melvyn No.2, Will and Pauline would discuss a big rebellion on their way home on a Sunday night – how to remove me, and make the group a social meeting place, and a social outreach centre. I remained convinced that commitment to Christ was the rock from which the tree would grow, and refused to shift, so that their opposition became more open and active. One of them would turn his chair round and face the other way when we were discussing, and some of the others took to saying that particular discussions were a waste of time. They did not like anything biblical, because it was 'too religious', and anything social/political was considered 'boring' because most contemporary matters were beyond their experience. I remember on one occasion recording an interview which the Prime Minister of the day gave about his faith, and the Christian ethic as he thought it applied to his busy job; I was accused of political bias, and told in no uncertain terms, and in their own choice phrases, that politics and religion do not mix! I was wearied by the whole thing; it seemed such a long time (over two years!) since I had begun this service for Christ, and I could see little or no fruit for my labours. Why should I keep giving up my precious time voluntarily to such an ungrateful rabble? When I thought I'd reached the end of my tether, I went to see Mr. Thompson, and he counselled me to keep trying just a little longer. I shall always be grateful for that piece of wisdom. For just three weeks later, the big breakthrough happened.

We had taken the Group to the Open Day at Cliff College in Derbyshire on Whit Monday for two successive years. Cliff is a Methodist College for training lay people in Christian work. It offered one year courses in evangelism, and had long been an evangelical power house in the British Methodist Church. Built in the stone of the Derbyshire hills in which it still stands, its rural peace and beauty are an inspiration to visitors. Every Whit Monday, many thousands of visitors from all parts of the United Kingdom came to its Open Day to hear some of the best preachers, men like David Watson, Gordon Bailey and Arthur Blessitt, in a series of outreach meetings in marquees and on the terrace. We grew to love the place, and hired the common room and chapel for a day conference on the 6th July. The theme was 'Vocation' and we asked two older Christians to talk about their own job, and how they could witness to Christ through it. One was a housewife, and the other a personnel manager in a large industrial works. What stuck out clearly was that, no matter how different their responsibilities, the sense of caring actively for the individual was part of their Christian calling. It was an inspiring day, culminating in a service in the College chapel, and in the reverent atmosphere of that wood-panelled, stained-glass windowed place, a call was made for those who wished to give their lives to Christ to come forward and kneel at the communion rail during the last hymn. Amid a flood of tears, Phil responded – he was to become a student of the College later, and his new found commitment was to take him for a time from his job with the N.C.B. into the Methodist ministry.

Love and friendship, and learning through discussion, were the seeds sown; Christ would reap the harvest of the years.

Other young people sat tightly in their seats, refusing to respond to what they saw to be the 'emotion' of the moment, though the emotion lay completely in their own decision not to respond, rather than in the calm and reasoned style of the preacher. We were disappointed, but not for long. The following evening at the Badminton Club, Will told me that he should have responded, and that he still wished to give his life to Christ. He was packed off to Mr. Thompson, where he sealed his decision in prayer. There followed a powerful struggle. Will and Melvyn No.2 were the best of friends, and walked to and from school together every day. Will's commitment was like a betrayal to Melvyn, a betrayal of their rebellion, and a betrayal of their innermost thoughts and fears. Melvyn expressed strongly at home that 'they' were not getting him, and his elder brother, Keith, a former Stanfield pupil and now working for Michelin, was convinced that 'the powers that be' (Youth leaders rather than God!) were after him. Will and Melvyn walked to and from school each day without speaking, and the atmosphere grew constantly more frozen. One Sunday night a few weeks later, Mal and Will decided to take Melvyn home, and, as soon as they were in the car, conversation began. By chance Michel Quoist's book "Prayers of life" lay open on the floor of the car at the prayer, "help me to say yes". It was read, and a car turned into a cathedral, as God' s silence descended. Melvyn was told that if he wished to give his life to Christ he should tell me at school the next day.

So on Monday morning I was crossing the entrance hall to go to the staff room, when an anxious figure threw back a classroom door, dashed down the corridor and tapped me gently on the shoulder. "I want to give my life to Christ." We prayed together, Will and Melvyn mended their friendship, and a new life began.

When eighteen of us went on the Group holiday to Guernsey that August, we took five new Christians. They were struggling with the adjustment of values necessary in a young Christian life. We were not without our problems (far from it!) but a new era had begun. One day there was a water fight on the lawns outside the chalets where we were staying. It was all good humoured and friendly fun, and most were dressed in trunks for it. I was in my most formal suit when Will ran up to me with a bowl of water. With the best authority of my teaching role I said, "You dare!" and he did; a teacher became a rather drowned friend.

Chapter 6
CASEY

I believe in Christian drama. The Church has long known it is an effective way of communicating the gospel, and I had always thought it sad that Church drama groups are satisfied with aping their secular counterparts in a series of farces, pantomimes and thrillers. Let the world do its own thing, I have long thought, and we'll do ours. We have few enough opportunities to present the truth of Christ to the non-Churchgoer. If we can get him into a theatre, we ought to tell him what we believe in an attractive and communicative way. Maybe we would win him, maybe we would challenge him, maybe we would only make him think more highly of Christians - but we would at least wake him up.

And for the cast, religious drama would be even more powerful. You could not be in a play without living it, eating it, drinking it. You must think through its ideas, you must interpret its characters. So you get to know what it wants to say, and you are never the same person afterwards. It is real teaching through experience.

These days I can explain what I then instinctively thought; then I was just struggling to find another practical outworking of the gospel, and happened to choose this one. Apart from 'Barrabas' and 'A Man born to be King', I had no experience of production. So I first chose a short forty minute play, "Casey" by Turner, with a small cast of nine. It's the story of a young soldier who gets into trouble with his girl friend, and finds the meaning of life in the love of the cross. In the modern idiom in those days, with a few songs scattered through, it really communicated. Phil was to be Casey, Paul the priest, and Trevor, a black guy. Drama was new to them too, and from this raw material came previously undiscovered talent. Melvyn No.2 was an old man, Adams, filled with thought of wars gone by, and capturing the mood of old age remarkably. I had really to work at rehearsals, because production was new to me, and acting to them. I learned, by process of trial and error, the value of firmness and confidence building. I made many mistakes, and had the annoying habit of changing my mind about moves just after the actors had learned them. But we had lots of laughs; Trevor regularly sent the cast into convulsions with a Negro spiritual, almost Al Johnson style, and we all enjoyed singing about "The good old "C of E" which "wafts us all to Heaven on a wave of parish tea" to the tune of "Marching through Georgia." Sylvia and Mal were leading lights in presenting a first half of modern gospel music with guitars, and, through this programme of music and drama, we made one new significant capture.

Rob hated school; he was in the fifth form, and was a constant source of trouble to staff, as he was to the local church he attended, where he and his friends created havoc, did much damage and were the despair of the brave local minister. Although intelligent, his attitude removed him from the opportunity of obtaining more than a minimum of '0' levels, and he had absolutely no direction to his life. But he was interested in drama, and he could play the guitar. I had a reasonable relationship with him (although there were times when he was angry with me too!) and after a series of only partially successful attempts to involve him, I invited him to be in "Casey". It was a sunny afternoon, he was sitting his last 'O' level exam, and he said yes. Every time he missed a rehearsal after that, preferring pub or club, I wrote him a letter reminding him of the next one, and it turned out right on the night.

We decide to use the old Wesley Place Church for the three evenings. It had not been in use for some months, and we had some difficulty in getting the piped heating to start again. We ripped out the front four rows of pews (with ministerial permission!) and removed the communion rail to make a stage area. Two spotlights were installed, and we cloaked off the children's chapel to represent the hill of Calvary. It was all crude and amateurish, but very exciting. Selling tickets wasn't easy. The congregation loyally supported us, though they dreaded what they might find, and friends and relatives were dragooned into accepting. We had an audience of a hundred for each of the first two nights, and a hundred and fifty for the third. The money was to be used to take a group of deprived children, referred to us by the N.S.P.C.C, on holiday. Social outreach had begun. The audience were, on the whole, appreciative. A member of our own Congregation wrote in the next Church magazine, "As one of the older members of the Church I should like to congratulate the Youth Group on the excellent concert they have given, and the good work they are doing. It is very gratifying to known that we have such a good company of young people in the Church."

Twenty five young people were involved in the production, and grease paint and sweat, laughter and music, gave us a reasonably polished production under appalling conditions. But more important, we discovered hidden talents, organisational, practical, dramatic, musical. Talents which in years to come would be of direct service to God.

Chapter 7

BARNES CLOSE

"Happiness is" was the title of a Youth Service we planned together for the Church one Sunday evening. In our preparation for it, every element of traditional worship came under close scrutiny. Why have a commercial break in the middle for notices and offertory? Wasn't the language of hymn and prayer outdated and too theological? Why not have several short talks instead of one long boring sermon?

So the formal service was scrapped; we tried to show what the world thought happiness was, drugs, sex, war, power, money, leisure, and then finally what the Christian thought. The congregation were to be asked to sit upstairs round the two front rows of the gallery, with the ground floor in darkness. We began with Ken Dodd singing 'Happiness' played on a record player, "Heaven forbid!!" Different members of the group read from newspaper cuttings, we had no organ, modern songs (and no hymns!), no notices, no offertory, one short prayer and no sermon. It was a disaster! Two old ladies refused to come upstairs and sat, lights switched off downstairs, in total darkness for the whole service. This was a real disturbance of the usual Chapel peace, and nearly everyone resented the wholesale destruction of their normal act of worship. The town buzzed with the scandal for a few days, but the young people remained happily oblivious. Mr. Thompson and I bore the criticisms for several weeks without passing them on to the Youth Group.

This occasion was important for one reason particularly. Rob No.2, another Stanfield pupil, had left school after a year in the lower sixth studying the sciences and tried to get in at a Further Education College. He wasn't successful; his girlfriend broke off their relationship and he returned to school to begin his sixth form course again, only doing Arts subjects this time. He was very mixed up, and not particularly happy, but he remembered the time when I had invited him to play his guitar and sing in a service called "Happiness Is". He sang the song "The war drags on" - and the song did - on and on and on. But some contact had been made, and Melvyn and Will persuaded him to come to the group. Bespectacled, with very long curly fair hair, very outspoken and apparently extrovert, he made quite an impact on our quieter churchgoers.

When we came to organise our first Group weekend conference, both he and Rob No.1 agreed to go without really realising what they might expect, as did a large body of our other members.

The weekend was to be spent at Barnes Close Conference Centre, near Birmingham. A large old house off the motorway, owned by the Birmingham Sunday School Union and hosted by Mr. And Mrs. Matthews, it had been the centre of Christian activities for many years.

Set in its own grounds and surrounded by countryside, it had a large lounge, kitchens and dining room, dormitory bedrooms, table tennis and billiard room. In the lounge, a fine carpeted room fitted out with arm chairs, a picture of Jesus dominated. Standing over the hearth, the searching whimsical eyes of Jesus followed you wherever you walked; 'And the Lord looked on Peter, and Peter remembered.' It was a homely but holy place.

To take a group of young people out of their home environment and centre their minds on the meaning and purpose of life is like putting a light to a stick of dynamite. As much goes on in informal discussion, particularly very late at night, as goes on in formal sessions. And the sharing of testimony is still the most powerful Christian force, as the early Church knew. Rev. Stanley Johnson was the speaker, and this time the personality of Jesus really came to life in minds prepared as he strode round as he talked, and with humour and bubbly persuasion kept the young people transfixed. At the Saturday evening social, Rob No.2 said to me, "I've been thinking about this Christianity thing. I must talk to you about it." But events beat him. On the Sunday morning before breakfast there was a communion service in the lounge. Anyone who did not want to take the bread and wine was still invited to attend, but not to hold their hands out when the server passed by. Several determined young pagans decided to kneel firm and not to receive, but as John Wesley said, communion is a converting ordinance, and in the struggle of pride and Holy Spirit, pride was defeated. For many of them it was the first time they had celebrated, and that tiny lump of bread and sip of wine seemed to smash down the barriers and open trembling hearts to the reception of the Lord.

That afternoon there was a final service. There had been much prayer and preparation over the months. One of the problems most evangelism faces, is that preparation and follow up are only patchy. There can be a shallow emotional response, or a real decision which fades through lack of Church support. We were not in that position. Will gave his public testimony for the first time and the atmosphere was electric. The chairs had been turned to face the bay window, and the picture of Christ was placed on a table. Those who wished to give their lives to Christ were asked to kneel on the floor at the front, and there was a series of heavy thuds throughout the hymn. Tears, clasped hands, bowed heads and earnest prayer, and then a long silence. The sense of the numinous was everywhere. God's presence seemed to fill the room, and we felt more inclined to whisper than to speak. Rob No.1 reported afterwards: "I hadn't decided to come forward, but somehow I felt myself drawn out, and before I knew where I was, I was kneeling at the front."

Although it is possible for people to grow gradually into the Christian faith, I believe there must be a moment for every Christian when he or she first consciously decides for Christ - the 'born again' experience. Not everyone can pinpoint the date, but there has to be a moment of entry into the Kingdom of God. Sadly, for many churchgoers, who are believers or God fearers, that experience has never happened. It really is flying in the face of the evidence to suggest that people can be converted without noticing it, or that some of them need no conversion at all. Conversion is made up of four elements: repentance, surrender, acceptance and a new direction. We have to be sorry for our inadequacy or unworthiness, our separation from God, our 'sin'. We need to hand over our lives, 'lock, stock and adventure' to Christ. We must accept the love and power of Christ into ourselves so that we may be, as Paul says, 'en Christo' (in Christ). And then we find a completely new way to walk had in hand with Him. To be 'soundly converted' as the old preachers would have it, all four must be true for us; then we will be in the Kingdom. So it seems right for the Church to create the opportunity to discover these truths in many different ways, though the public response in the context of an act of worship seems one of the most effective. After all, when Jesus called men and women during his ministry, he made them show their allegiance to him both privately and publicly, and when anyone says to me "I don't know whether I'm a Christian or not because I haven't made such a conscious decision", I suggest that they go home, kneel by their beds, and with no prejudice against what is past, fully and consciously offer their life to Christ and accept His indwelling power, and then go out and publicly demonstrate this private decision, maybe at first just by telling the person it is most difficult to tell, but certainly then by living the life of a Christian.

For these young people, this moment had come, and they were to know the transforming experience of the light of Christ breaking into the darkness of their souls, so that their world was turned upside down, never to be the same again.

Eight young people responded during that final service, including the two Robs, and Phil's younger brother, Dave. But Keith, Gill and Pauline and a young, fair haired, Sandra, sat firmly in their seats, and went for a rebellious smouldering walk in the grounds immediately afterwards. For the two Robs it was a traumatic experience, and they were to take time to sort out their new moral and social attitudes. But Christ does change people as nothing else can.

Nor was this the end of this particular chapter. During the week following, Keith, Pauline and Sandra each made their way to the Manse to express their readiness to accept Christ, and to receive Him in prayer. Mr. Thompson often had tears in his eyes as with shaky voice he led a young life into the Kingdom.

Chapter 8
THE BREEZE RUSTLES

What was the Church to make of this vigorous, excited young life? Worship seemed suddenly meaningful, and lusty young throats pounded out the hymns, bowed heads were reverent in prayer, positive sermon criticism was argued through as ideas were sorted out. We moved from the back pew upstairs, to the front pews downstairs, and usually on a Sunday evening there were more than twenty of us. We were noticeable, but there seemed many blind eyes. The minister and his wife were tremendous; the Manse was always an open house, and on many occasions I sent young people to Mr. Thompson for advice, knowing they would receive a warm welcome and a good dose of spiritual wisdom. Mrs. Thompson had a free flow of natural conversation, and many a young person would be regaled with funny stories of when she and Claude were young, and treated to coffee and biscuits, while he waited to take them into his study.

Church membership became what it should always have been - the natural follow-through from Christian commitment - so membership classes were held with increasing frequency in the Manse. As is Methodist practice, all new members should be attached to a class meeting with a class leader who is pastorally responsible for his members, and in the great revival days of Methodism both band and class meetings met regularly. Meetings had ceased to be held a long time before this in our Church, so when I was invited to be class leader of the new members, I made two provisos: first, that it was the duty of each member to attend my class meeting regularly, and second that I did not have to collect 'class money', which seemed to me to be a denial of the spiritual role of the classes in favour of getting more money for the Church. My class was a mixture of folk Christian and thinking themselves Christian, and included Alan, who had been converted at Barnes Close and was a member of a local United Reformed Church, but had no fellowship meeting to attend there. On that first Wednesday meeting in our front room, I read to them from Dr. Sangster's "Methodism can be born again", first printed in March 1938. He wrote about true Christian fellowship thus:

"In the Kingdom of God on earth, the bond that mattered most would be the common faith, the common experience, the common Lord. Whosoever did the will of God would be His brother and sister - and mother! The family life of believers would cut across the accident of parentage, and be composed of those who had made the same surrender, and were committed to the same cause. In these small cells of vital spiritual life, the

deepest fellowship would be realised. Living within the Larger Body of the Church, on whose strength they drew, in part, for sustenance, and to the maintenance of which they gave their life, these small organisms would grow in spiritual power, and made possible the highest life of the members composing them. The word 'fellowship' can only be known at its best in this relationship. Above the handful, fellowship necessarily loses depth. There is a fellowship of a real kind when the whole local Church meets for worship, but it is a different fellowship. Rich reciprocity is not possible: the inter-play of minds is limited: a multitude of people cannot live in each others lives: we are facing again the limitations of human nature, and must recognise that fellowship gets thinner the wider it spreads.

In its early days, Methodism had this fellowship in an extraordinary degree...... They called the cells 'classes' and every member, met in class..... In these little groups, the spiritual quest was pursued with passion. Holiness was the aim, a holiness which was often too individualistic, and ignored social injustice, but which necessarily carried the seeds of this wider interpretation of the gospel in it - seeds that were to grow in subsequent generations. The equality of family life prevailed. Prayer, praise, confession, witness, teaching - all had their place. Members were expected to speak. It was felt to be dishonouring to God to be dumb in His praise, and disloyal to the fellowship not to give as well as get, and dangerous to the soul to stifle confession when the Spirit of God moved one to it. So they grew in grace and exulted in a fellowship, so rich and deep, that difference of age, learning and social standing were as nothing to them, and these golden hours became an 'antepast of heaven'."

I definitely could not have expressed these ideas with such clarity, but it was towards such fellowship that I wanted the class meeting to move. I was very much the leader in those early days; not able to share my inner self, because leaders aren't supposed to have feelings or problems; giving rather than getting. But all that was to change. As our fellowship grew deeper, so I became increasingly an equal member, so that the class meeting became for me my saving grace, as a young Christian who had never before known real fellowship. It still surprises me how often as Christians we wear masks to disguise our real selves from fellow Christians. But maybe it is because we need more trust, and trust comes with continuous practice, and only with a small group of people. Most Christians have never had that practice, have never met with such people. Many Christians mistake brotherliness, that family sense which binds us together, for fellowship; fellowship includes that of course, but it is so much more. The physical isolation of many solitary Christians, and the failure of the Churches to provide real meeting points, both these weaken the Church. And in a society where loneliness is endemic, we need to re-discover that vital oneness which made an early observer of the Church say, "See how these Christians love one another." Our class meeting shared the deepest most personal things, because we had grown to love and trust one another in Christ. Not that we had arrived, for there was always further to go, but we were trying to move.

I was a local preacher; that meant I was responsible for conducting worship and preaching in my own locality, twenty odd churches of Tunstall Circuit, a calling which gave great opportunity for evangelism. I found that God soon started calling my young friends in a remarkable and ever increasing way to become preachers themselves. I remember one night at a play rehearsal being button-holed by Rob and Rob separately and independently, "Could I have a word with you?" One after the other they confessed their sense of God's calling, and neither knew the other's thought. But Phil preceded them, a preacher on note with me for six months, learning the tricks of the trade, but teaching me much about preaching and worship-leading too! And then there was Melvyn No.2, shyness and silence disappearing under pressure from the Holy Spirit, finding a real gift for humour and illustration. We had a real ministry together, he and I, during his six months 'on note' with me. We complemented each other, and the Holy Spirit spoke to congregations in our charge.

At Packmoor Chapel we sang "Lord of the Dance" together, and taught it to the children; nor were we disturbed when a little girl, unable to get off an Anniversary stage quickly enough, had an accident probably through nerves, and the pulpit was nearly awash! When we met together to plan, we would often start from a theme, drift far from it in conversation and find God's guidance in a meandering talk. And we seemed especially called to 'sock the gospel' to our hearers. More of that anon.

Each quarter Mr. Thompson was able to present to the local preachers' meeting another two or three names to be given a note to preach, and that in a circuit which had seen only the very occasional new preacher over very many years!

It was amazing how the growth of the group seemed divinely planned. As the number of Christians increased, so the general numbers increased, so that we were always able to keep a balance of Christians and non-Christians. People who came to the Sunday evening sessions were struck by the warmth of the welcome, and the love and friendship which seemed so out of tune with their experience elsewhere. And the new babes in Christ were enthusiastic, often aggressive, in their invitations. By the summer of 1970 there were over 60 regular attending members, and we transferred our venue to the main hall. It was often imagined by outsiders that these were all the 'nice religious' young people of the neighbourhood – far from it! Most of them were unchurched, there were some from denominations Catholic to Brethren, and only a very few came from established Methodist channels. In fact our intake into the Church was composed largely of those who came from little or no Church background at all, and they found Methodist worship and organisation strange and rather dead. And our regular worshipping congregation found the newcomers strange too, guys with long hair, and dressed in jeans, and the girls in maxi skirts; their appearance hid their devotion and obvious attention to the service.

Because we were now so much larger, we could not hold an effective discussion when we were all together, so we decided to split into groups, which met on a rotation basis in each of the little chapel vestries, as some were more dirty and untidy than others. It meant I needed helpers to lead discussions – so I invited the established Christians and some of the newer ones too, two to a group, and gradually evolved in my own mid the criteria on which to do it. I often made mistakes, but I found that responsibility is great for young Christians – it concentrates the mind wonderfully. Much leadership potential was realised, as the number of leaders available always seemed to balance with the numbers attending. People were by now coming from all over the city and further afield, often travelling for eight to twelve miles to get to "The Group" as it became known. We ran a car ferry service, loading our cars two or three times an evening to take people home, and often finishing after eleven o'clock at night.

Amidst all this activity it was amazing how blind many members of the Church could be. They perhaps imagined an orgy of table tennis and snogging on a Sunday night, and took the process of powerful public testimonies, regular membership services, and new faces among the local preachers with scarcely a blink of the eye. In fact, when the group had grown even larger and its activities increased, a regular worshipper who had received a letter from a visitor congratulating him on the exciting things going on in his Church, was heard to ask bewilderedly what was going on, because he hadn't noticed anything!

Chapter 9

ACTIVITIES - SPIRITUAL

From 1970 onwards, the number of conversions gathered momentum to such an extent that it became impossible to keep in touch completely. In the most unlikely places, often with the most unlikely people, near at hand and far afield, under the most unlikely circumstances, so that our initial delight and emotion at every one turned into a sort of desperate duty to see that everyone was helped. I cannot possibly list here the very many involved. The parable of the unleavened bread spoke to our situation, because the yeast bubbles and ferments as it spreads through the dough. Perhaps even more descriptive is the pebble in the pond which causes ripples spreading to the further extremities of the waters. So I will select a few stories. For each ripple is like another pebble causing a new series of ripples of its own.

At Stanfield, Keith No.1 belonged to a group of lads whose attitude to life was cynical, and jeering. His '0' level results dictated his choice of 'A' levels which included R.E. Although he was fairly knowledgeable, his interest never appeared to go beyond the academic, and he applied to University to study Sociology. I well remember that on the last occasion I saw his teaching group, I took them to Leek to see a Bible exhibition. Driving him home, I stopped the car for him to get out. He turned to me. "Sir, do you know anything about Ghandi?" "That he was a man of peace, lived in India, had a high moral code," I said as an opener, "Why do you ask?" "I've been reading a book about him. He was a tremendous chap. I want to know more about him. He'd got a reason for living." I pointed him to the public library, and as he got out of the car, I regretfully thought that this seed of interest was something I could do nothing about.

But he failed his 'A' levels, much to the staff's surprise. And he returned for a third year, inwardly broken. Melvyn and Will befriended him and brought him to the group where he would argue for hours, well into the night, sitting in front of the coal fire in the bottom room, about the philosophical basis of Christianity. He was not a Church goer and did not see the relevance of the Church, but the person of Jesus fascinated him, and he was drawn despite himself. One Sunday Melvyn and I were invited by a local minister to put the claims of commitment to Christ firmly to the congregation of Stanfield Methodist Chapel, and Keith decided to attend, long haired, in scruffy jeans and pumps. My sermon came out as God intended, and not as I did, and it was moving to see Keith kneeling at the communion rail alone to give his life to Christ. This decision became the driving force of his life. He married a Christian girl, Sylvia, and went to Wesley House, Cambridge studying for his Ph.D. in

Church History and training for the Methodist Ministry; his eldest daughter while still small took her own opportunity to "Praise de Lord"!

It was Monday night at the Badminton Club, and I was in the choir vestry discussing with Melvyn No.2's elder brother, Keith, why his brother had got religion. He believed in God, but it had little or nothing to do with his life. And when he went away on a Michelin sandwich course to Salford University, Melvyn and I made a pact to pray for him, and persuaded Mr. Thompson to write to the local chaplain to ask him to visit. He did, but it was the Navigators who really succeeded. Their persistent friendliness led to a quiet declaration of faith, and brought him to the Group when he came home for the holidays. Another day Conference was held at Cliff College, and a service in the College chapel gave him the opportunity quietly but determinedly to commit his life to Christ. That was a very special day Conference for me for other reasons. My youngest brother Philip had started coming to the group at the lower age limit, 14. He was still only a boy then, and liked to kick a football round the main room, or snowball cars as they were leaving on Sunday night. He did not like discussions; he never said anything. And eventually he just stopped coming. Encouragement from friends brought him back again, and one Sunday night we were in discussion, when he whispered to me his opinion. "Philip wants to say something" I announced to the Group, and very haltingly he was in with both feet. I was myself preaching in Cliff chapel on that same day Conference, and made the call to commitment. When bodies dumped themselves unceremoniously at the Communion rail, I inwardly rejoiced, but when Philip came out I was completely overcome and could hardly pronounce the benediction. To have a brother who is a brother in Christ!

A joint C.E.M. Conference with the local girls grammar school provided three of the Stanfield lads with a wonderful opportunity for witness. "We know Jesus Christ as our personal Saviour. Christ is alive. He has changed our lives," and to three girls separately, "Why don't you come along to the Group to find out more." Melvyn, Will and Keith were in the forefront as Group evangelists and three came. They each have their story, but I choose to tell you about Lis. She was an Anglican, brought up in the Church, with a very strong faith, but concerned about this commitment thing. "Surely you don't have to do something as public and dramatic as everyone at the Group claims! It's very Methodist. Not Anglican at all." But on the day Conference at Cliff, the first person out in the first line of the hymn, like a bolt from the blue, hurled to the front, was Lis.

But sometimes, the miracles happened during a normal Church service in quite unexpected circumstances. One young man gave his life to Christ during a Sunday School Anniversary, and another on Ladies

Sunday! Sometimes God takes hold of his preachers, and makes them behave as He requires, which is completely different than what they had prepared. A local preacher who should have taken Ladies Sunday was taken ill at the last moment, and a middle aged lady came in her place, a preacher for many years, who had never made an appeal for commitment before. In the service was David, a server from the local Anglican Church, who could not find the answers to the questions he asked among his own local congregation, and had come to the Group as a searcher. On that particular Sunday night, he had come to Church with a certain inner knowledge that he would there and then give his life to Christ. The lady preacher had the overwhelming sense that she must make a call. She was so embarrassed by it that she got the words wrong: "Will anyone who is a Christian come and stand at the front here with me?" It was surprising the whole congregation did not move, but it was David who responded.

On one occasion Mr. Thompson was visited by a girl who was confused spiritually, but whom he decided needed the opportunity to make a decision. So the following Sunday night he provided it. "The girl who I know wishes to make a decision for Christ may now take that opportunity if she wishes." In an instant, seven girls had left their places to kneel at the front. "If only I had mentioned boys!" he used to say.

Hilary and Rosemary were identical twins, and their best friend was Helen with whom they had grown up. A group of students from Cliff College came to the Church to take a weekend mission, and on the Saturday night, as twins will, they both responded to a call. They were so excited, they had to ring their friend Helen, who had just gone away to University. "Just before you tell me your news," she said, "I'd just like to tell you I've become a Christian this weekend!"

On one occasion I was asked to take a straight - forward service of worship in a Methodist Chapel outside the Circuit. When I arrived, twenty minutes early, there were three or four old ladies in the congregation, and I spent my time in the vestry thinking the whole thing did not promise to be very uplifting. At service time I walked into the pulpit, looked out on a surprisingly large congregation, and noticed Anne, who had been coming to the Group for a few weeks, sitting with her mother. I had an immediate sense that I should scrap my prepared sermon, preach for commitment, and that Anne would respond. I struggled with this feeling, throughout the service, half of me saying I was imagining it, but giving in to it at the end. Words for the sermon seemed to come from nowhere, and I screwed up the courage to make the appeal. Sure enough, she, and two other girls came and knelt at the front. How wonderful God is! In many such ways the Lord often demonstrated His Sovereignty.

One night I was at home watching television when Ian rang me. "I've been talking to Cath on the phone", he said, "and she wants to make a decision for Christ. But she doesn't know what to do. What should I tell her?" "Tell her to kneel at the bedside, and, in prayer, hand her life over to Christ and invite Him in," I said, "and then make it public by telling someone she would find it difficult to tell." It was almost like switching on a tape recorder, except that the concern was real. I spent the next few minutes in prayer. The phone rang, "She's done it," he said, "Praise the Lord!"

Alan had been in trouble both in and out of school. He was very intelligent and sensitive, but was mixed up by adolescence, and liked to throw his weight about. But he sometimes shared his problems, and when he left the Lower Sixth to go to a Further Education College I felt we would hear more of him. We did.

It was the end of the day, and I was finishing a lesson in division form four when the door burst open, and Rob No.2 stood there red faced and emotional, "Could you come with me, Sir, now?" I followed him meekly down the corridor to find Alan, in tears, hands clutched together, "Please help me to become a Christian. I want to be a Christian" he pleaded. Apparently he had paid a courtesy visit to school and had found Rob working on the stage. They had never got on well together, but they started talking, and Rob told him the story of his conversion. There was one of those hushed moments when it seemed as if the spirit of God reached down and touched his heart, and now here he was begging to be converted! We prayed together and he committed his life to Christ. I gave him some practical, baby Christian, advice including a scrap of paper with the words "for God so loved the world that he gave His only Son that whoever believes in Him may not die but have everlasting life" scribbled on, and he was gone. I never saw him again. Outwardly he showed no signs of his experience. He did not go to Church; he did not openly live the Christian life. I heard he had gone to College of Education, and then he was killed in a road accident. I often used to pray that his name may be written in heaven.

Chapter 10

AND SOCIAL

This country is a mission field. The root of all her problems, political, social, economic, it seems to me, is loss of faith. Not that people don't believe in God. Polls have often shown that the majority of British people accept the existence of the Almighty. But that personal experience of Jesus Christ, that burning living faith which the Bible offers is lost to the majority. And the trouble was that in the seventies and eighties we still talked of living in a Christian country. Most people used to claim to be Christian. But they meant by that, that they were living reasonably decent lives, or were kind to their family and little children, or had some element of social concern, or went to Church regularly, or believed in God. And yet Christ tells us that none of these things make a man a Christian. Not that He ever used the word "Christian." That was a nickname attached to His disciples after His death – the "Christ-ians", whose lives were centred on Christ. According to the Synoptic Gospels, he talked more about what was involved in belonging to the Kingdom of God, and He didn't mean Heaven. Membership of the Kingdom was a "there and then" (or "here and now") experience. You were either in it or you weren't. You could be near to it by your standard of life or your faith, but you could only be in it by such a reversal of your values that you came first to love God with all your heart and soul and mind and strength, and second to love your neighbour. Anyone who has really grappled with himself, with his hopes and fears, his selfishness and pride, will agree that this reversal requires some extra power if it is to be achieved. The Christian code is too impossibly high for us to maintain in our own strength alone. And that is why membership of the Kingdom involves surrender of one's self to Jesus, and an acceptance of His power into one's life. He taught His disciples that when He had gone He would give them His Spirit to bring love and meaning and power to their lives. Those who were 'born again' into the Kingdom would know that power; those who weren't, wouldn't. And most modern Western civilised men don't. What changes would come to society if only individual men and women came to know the living power of Jesus in their lives!

Each 'Christian' is only such because he was first aware of the inadequacy and emptiness of his own life, a 'sense of sin' as the nineteenth century preacher would have called it. This hopeless, despairing situation would lead to a search, which could never be satisfied by drugs or sex or booze or lust for power, but only by a personal experience of Jesus. And Jesus promised that when we really needed Him, we had only to ask and He would come in. So in the simplest act of prayer, by the bedside, in the church, on the 'bus, anywhere, it is possible to say something like, "Dear Jesus, I know I can't manage on my own. I need you to make my life complete. I give myself to you. I surrender all that I have and am at the foot of your cross. I accept your power into my life. Come and live in me and make me new, Amen," and know that your prayer would be heard and answered. So we can each enter the Kingdom.

Every person Jesus called in the days of His earthly life had to make both a private and public response. So it is today still necessary for every new convert to give himself privately to the Lord, and to show by some act of public witness that his is now the King's man. So in the Youth Group we made witness one of the six counselling points carefully explained to any new 'babe in Christ'. Begin by telling someone you would find it difficult to tell, and then make your life and your words bear witness to your faith.

We also advised regular worship in their own Church, or at the Church in Tunstall if they belonged nowhere else; the need to be with the community of Christ's people was coupled with the need for regular fellowship. Mal's meet became an eight week training ground for young Christians. They then joined membership classes, led by the Minister, and then joined in a class meeting, a regular fortnightly time of sharing on a Wednesday. The number of these grew over the years, but they each had about 15 – 20 members. Private devotions are important too, so teaching on how to pray, and advice on regular Bible study were part of our programme. And because a conversion experience includes emotion, we reminded our converts that man is made up of emotion, intellect and will, and that just because we do not always feel 'high', it does not mean we are far from God – we should rely on faith, and not on feelings.

Concern for others stems out of love of God as far as the Christian is concerned. Jesus got His commandments in the right order of priority, and any programme for Christian action should begin with man's spiritual needs and with his response to God. But it cannot stop there. For commitment affects every part of life, social, moral, political, economic, and the Kingdom becomes the corporate caring of individual members as they exercise together the principles of Christian living.

It wasn't long before the needs of the world became the indignant concern of the babes in Christ. Why spend money on vast Cathedrals when there are babies dying of starvation in the streets of Calcutta? Who cares about the lonely and house-bound? Why does God allow suffering, and how can we meet the needs of the physically and mentally handicapped? Much of their response to these concerns found expression through social service schemes in College and University, through individual caring for the neighbour down the street, and through the careful stewardship of their money. David, for example, chose to begin a visitation scheme for elderly people in the community and we cooked them a Christmas day dinner each year. That was a chaotic affair. Much willing help, old fashioned cookers and utensils, bleeding fingers from opening tins, badly co-ordinated timing, much peeling of sprouts, and frantic journeys in Meals on Wheels vans were a lively way to begin December 25th. It was the faces of the elderly which had most impact: "My first Christmas dinner for fifteen years" an old lady exclaimed with delight! We also took them fruit and vegetables from the Church's Harvest and met the same response. And when at Christmas we organised a party for deprived children recommended to us by the N.S.P.C.C. we began to realise the responsibility of caring. Children who don't know love and are desperate to get it, and the personality problems this creates, are a real challenge to a teenager. We raised money, gained grants, and took groups of them away camping or living in Church halls for a week at a time to Prestatyn or the Lake District or even further afield. Bed wetting and refusal to eat, sulkiness and fights, were all cheerfully coped with, and for many children for whom it was their first real holiday, it was an unforgettable experience. Packing the tents up, soggy and bedraggled, one windswept day in the Lake District, we looked round at the cheery, excited, healthy children, and privately agreed that our own exhaustion was well worthwhile. They were to remember the holiday and the relationships it made, for years to come.

I was just as concerned to provide social activities for the young people themselves as they were to see the social needs of others met. Hikes were always popular, and 'Mal's walks' became infamous among the sufferers. For some reason it always rained. I remember on one occasion taking a 'short cut' up a hill when the heavens opened and it snowed a blizzard. Then every following hill we had to climb only revealed another summit to conquer. Girls lost their shoes in thick black squelchy oozing mud, and, as we picked our way sightless in single file along the top of a mountain ridge, the sheep were almost literally dying around us as we walked round a headland until we were miles from any signs of civilisation. Then the heavens opened and we stood on a cliff overlooking the sea, fifteen people under each umbrella, singing hymns, and soaked to the skin. On another previous holiday walk we were so absolutely wet through that when we reached a village the boys changed into their bathing trunks in the public toilets and travelled back on the bus semi-nude!

An annual holiday also became a natural regular feature: Scotland - Guernsey - Cornwall - Devon - St. Andrews - Aberystwyth - Exeter and so on. We graduated from tents, through caravans and chalets, to a maladjusted children's home, a university hall of residence, and finally then to university flats, self sufficient and free. And the numbers attending grew from eleven to over eighty. Put a group of young people together for a fortnight and you throw up problems faster than you can solve. New relationships made, old ones dissolved, the freedom from parental ties, the need to establish identity, all make fascinating situations. Our holidays quickly took on a spiritual flavour. Epilogues, open air witness on the beach or prom, bible study and, group discussion, our own services or attending a local lively Church (rather than just a 'Methodist one.') and late night prayer meetings were all a feature. We came to call them 'join-in' holidays, and those who came agreed to be involved in all the 'join-in' activities – though there was plenty of free time. Different members of the group organised different activities – a visit to a cinema or theatre, a bus trip, a discussion or an epilogue. And a real atmosphere of communal togetherness was created.

Many incidents were memorable, such as our own crocodile of eighty young holiday makers noisily processing through a town on a Sunday morning to overwhelm the congregation of a local church. In Ilfracombe, we took part in their mid-week mission service which was broadcast into the street, singing and giving testimony and handing out leaflets; then we marched through the streets still singing and chanting jubilantly, to the amazement of the locals. In Sidmouth we held open air services on the green, and when it rained, entertained and challenged a group of people waiting for a bus in the nearest bus shelter. In St. Andrews we grew to love the warmth of the welcome of the local Baptist Church. At Aberystwyth University we had free use of the chapel, and attracted and amazed an Anglican vicar on holiday. In Cornwall we had our morning Sunday Service on the cliff tops overlooking the sea, and as we praised God for the glory of His creation with "Summer suns are glowing over land and sea," the sun broke through the cloudy skies and streamed down upon us.

The summer holiday was invariably the time for 'O' level or 'A' level results for some of our members. Increasing tension seized people differently. Some were impatient to know, some feigned unconcern, and others wanted to run away and hide! For several years I had the job of ringing through to a central point at home to gather the results together, and of taking aside each pale-faced examinee and breaking the news. On one occasion, I had to chase those who would rather not know round a busy town before I could tell them. And I remember causing complete confusion in a coffee bar in Plymouth bus station where the thronged multitude cheered and yelled and laughed and flung their arms around each other in tears of joy.

Holidays usually seemed tinted golden, and it was always down to earth with a bump when our coaches arrived back to the familiar sight of the grey face of Tunstall tower square clock. On the final Saturday evening of the last two or three holidays we opened up the Church in Tunstall for a very unconventional thanksgiving service, attended by holiday makers, parents and friends. These were fairly basic gospel laugh-ins, and helped parental ties enormously. Not that we did not have golden experience at home. Many of our social occasions had the same tint of laughter and freedom, and stood out as red letter days in the annual calendar. We organised an annual 'join-in' at Christmas time - a really large buffet, games and dancing in the Town hall or the Park Floral Hall. The day was spent in hanging decorations, organising the P.A. system, and filling vol-au-vents, and the pace and atmosphere of a crowded evening set the scene for Christmas. On December 31st each year, we followed good Methodist practice by organising a Watchnight Social and Service for the whole Church. This was an opportunity for quickly prepared sketches and music, a sort of gentle satire of world and Church. We dressed in drag, took the mickey out of the minister, and generally enjoyed ourselves. The service was always one of the most powerful and moving of the year. I particularly remember Mr. Thompson speaking forcefully to those of the Church whose Christian commitment may have lost its way:" Go back to the place where you started, remember what you did there, and begin again with God," he said. Christian wisdom for the beginning of a new year.

Chapter 11
TOUCHSTONE

"It completely changed my life." The little old lady stood on the doorstep triumphantly, "I found what it really was to believe." The subject was a youth group play, and the young caller addressed was rather dazed to discover that his personal performance had had such a profound effect. But that's Christian drama for you. It cuts through years of agnosticism with an incision which leaves traditional methods of approach gasping.

After "Casey" our next attempt at drama, was "Jo Jonah" by Colin Hodgetts, using the small upper hall and stage at Pittshill Methodist Chapel. Jo Jonah is the epitome of modern man with his little box on the hillside, living a blinkered life, which refuses to see the suffering of a large part of the world even when God thrusts it at him. And yet he can't escape; God's love pursues him until he turns to meet the uncaring world himself, and becomes himself rejected by those who don't want to see.

This was a lively musical play, but, after it was over, I discovered that good religious drama was hard to find. So the following year I found myself adapting a very old script to produce the play "Cankerapple". It concerned the devil of that name and his young assistant Wart, who was challenged by the scenes of faith from Christian history, and eventually betrayed his master to kneel at the cross. It contained much humour, and the Devil didn't seem to like being laughed at. A series of disasters nearly engulfed the production. A sore throat bug spread like wild-fire; the roof of the main hall started to collapse and had to be reinforced at the eleventh hour; bangers in bottles were thrown in to the porch by the hall to startle and alarm the audience during the production. But the most memorable thing about the production was the song written by Rob. I had been sitting in the Youth Centre, turning over in my mind how to finish the play, and had decided that we needed an original song of commitment when Sandy come running up to me: "Brian, come and hear what Rob's written!" And in another room he played me that song which expressed his own experience, and which became the moving end to 'Cankerapple.'

> "All that I possess my Lord has given to me,
> Lips that I may bless and eyes that I may see
> The Glory of the Lord
> Which cannot be ignored,
> And He helped me to feel
> His love so strong and real."

This was the very first verse of his new found ability to write Christian music.

Rob was to sing the whole song many times, but could never do so without feeling the presence of God both then, and, like that silver thread, running through his life; to sing it became in itself a spiritual experience. And it gave me my idea. The following year I decided to write my own play, and to ask Rob to write songs as part of it. "Gospel Truth" was the result, the story of three youths in trouble with the law for breaking into a warehouse and assaulting the night watchman. One of them, played by the other Rob, was a dreamer who could not make relationships, with his mother, his employer, or his girl friend, and sought refuge in the anonymity of the gang or the football crowd. The court knew the truth that he had committed this crime, but the heavenly court tempered justice with mercy, and saw the reason for his sins and gave him the gospel as his salvation from the situation. The chorus played a football crowd, and really enjoyed themselves emulating Stoke City Boothen End. And we were in the Mitchell Memorial Theatre, Hanley, for the first time. Built for youth work in memory of Reginald Mitchell, the city man who invented the Spitfire, it had a magnificent stage, workshop and dressing rooms, and a cosy auditorium for 400 people. We built the set, collected the props, house managed, sold our printed programmes and made and served coffee in the interval. We were not allowed to operate the lights, which were in the charge of the resident electrician, Len Heath, with whom good relationships were developed over the years. But the surroundings improved our professionalism, and brought us larger and more enthusiastic audiences. Rob, our composer, could neither write nor read music, and his tunes were composed in his head, and taught directly to choir and guitarists. But he and I developed an understanding which must have been of God. It became impossible to see any difference of style and approach in the plays and their music, and over the years he would write songs while away at University from a few scrappy notes of mine, and compose words for songs which would often re-quote what I had written although he had never seen the script. As I finished each play, as though by magic a new title and subject would appear. I always took this as an indication that I was to continue writing. So "Gospel Truth" was followed by "The Triton's Horn," "Any Other Name," "Now or Never," and "Fisherman John" and so on. At the time of writing, thirteen plays are current.

Our audiences seemed to come from further afield all the time. As the members of the group moved away to College or University so they brought back bus loads of students, often wildly enthusiastic, some of whom were to find their way to Christ through the message of the play. We always managed to find room for a large cast, and gave ample opportunity for choir and crowd or chorus to make their mark on the play. And we had our usual crises. The power strike, and restrictions on the use of electricity threatened the whole production one year, and on another occasion a really heavy snowstorm almost prevented our electrician from arriving. After the first night of "Now or Never," Trevor, who was playing one of the lead parts, completely lost his voice, and I had to step in with a few hours notice, rehearsing the moves on stage only a couple of hours before I walked on, and struggling through a part written better than it was acted. But on every occasion we depended on the Lord. Each play figured high in our prayers, and before each performance we would meet together in the girls' dressing room to offer Him in prayer our attempt at witness and to ask Him to empower it. For Christian drama is as empty as any other witness unless it is infused by the power of the Holy Spirit. And on every occasion it was not so much the words or the tunes of the play which impressed, as the enthusiasm and sincerity of the cast. "As I was watching the play" observers would often say, "I wondered where all that joy came from, and what was missing from my life that I didn't have it."

Young people learn self discipline through drama, they discover more about themselves, they come to have confidence, and they enjoy the excitement and the challenge of working together in a team. But, most important, they know the real fulfilment of standing for Jesus publicly, and offering His gospel to others. And that's why we became known as "Touchstone" for a period. As our drama group grew, so we looked for a name that would express our reason for existence. The philosopher jester of Shakespeare's "As You Like It" glossed over his deep understanding of the reality of the human condition with humour and pathos; and George Herbert's hymn "Teach me my God and King in all things Thee to see" reminded us of the stone of old which turned all to gold. Herbert saw that the Christian faith, the reality of Christ, was just like this stone. And we came to hope that our performance would turn to gold the daily experience of each individual in the audience:

> "This is the famous stone
> That turneth all to gold,
> For that which God doth touch and own
> Cannot for less be told."

Chapter 12

BUILDING BRIDGES

"Many meetings, but not much meeting," is a faithful Church servant's weary comment. But meetings flooded the Youth Group week, often with a healthy informality, and absence of stuffy agenda and resolution. On one occasion Melvyn and Will approached me with an air of seriousness. "Isn't it about time we started to pray for our work? And can't we study the Bible more deeply? And what are we doing to witness to our faith to the outside world?" And so three more meetings were born.

The prayer meeting began in the back vestry at Jubilee, a long narrow room, wood panelled, with pews round the walls, Hugh Bourne's first pulpit, and a leather covered table. We met on a Wednesday fortnightly, and Mr. Thompson took the lead. Open prayer was an absolutely new experience to our young converts as it nearly was to me. And it could not just be offered in the conventional language of the old Methodist revival hour. These were modern men and women, who knew the language of the pub or club better than Wesley's journals, and they expressed themselves with directness and common sense. "I'm fed up with myself, Lord. I do such stupid things, I want to be better for you, but I keep getting in the way. Help me please. Amen." Often short and sweet, sometimes long and pleading, these prayers filled the silences for an hour or so, and, as the numbers grew and the seats were full, we sat on the table and the floor, and bodies crouching in prayer touched one another. When there were thirty five of us we moved into the Church and knelt around the communion rail, and a real sense of holiness filled the air. But somehow, when Jubilee was closed, we lost this sense, and a staid formality punctuated with long silences crept in. So we scrapped our meeting, and turned to cells, small groups meeting weekly in one another's homes. There is so much to learn about prayer, and I knew that at this time we were only timidly feeling the water. But I knew too that our work would only grow through prayer, and that God always answers, so I always tried to keep prayer at the centre of the life of the Group.

"There's a group of young people in Tunstall who you'll find are very fundamentalist, narrow and judgmental", a visiting minister was once told. Nothing could be further from the truth. The idea that we were rather sober and straightlaced, even if this were a true criticism of certain sections of the Church (which I doubt) is a real misconception of a group of young, trendy pagans finding the Bible and its theology to be a bombshell shattering their previous manners and morals. How mistaken we often are in the Church when we bring our great debates about the truth of the Bible down (or up) to the level of those who are turning its pages for the first time. I refuse to be labelled a "fundamentalist" or a "liberal"; I am a Christian, and I desire only to fight for Christ in the world. The Bible studies we held were primarily devotional; of course we were taught, and of course we argued. But we went to be fed, and a circle of longhairs and jeans and direct stammering questions does not want, is not ready, for the niceties of realised eschatology, or divine empiricism. We proclaimed our certainties to one another and were kind and careful with our doubts.

But the most dramatic of our 'meetings' were the open air services. The venue was Tunstall Park on a Sunday afternoon at three o'clock. We took an old rickety chair, placed it below the old bandstand, on an area of grass overlooking the tennis courts, someone stood on it and delivered, and on average fifty or sixty others stood round and sang and prayed silently. I remember Mr. Thompson standing there waving his arms to the singing, as the guitarists plucked their way through Youth Praise; I remember those young people who stood there week after week to give testimony in public for the very first time, sometimes so quietly and haltingly that they had to be prayed through, sometimes confidently expressing their unwilling suitability for preaching; it was often moving, even though sometimes the numbers who stopped to listen were discouraging. But we never knew how far we reached. People from the houses in the road which ran alongside the park told us that they put their deckchairs out so they could listen; the park-keeper listened to us at the other end of the park, so we knew we were widely heard, and a group of aimless young people, some from the Tunstall gangs, gathered regularly on the bandstand to throw abuse and laughter and stones. On one occasion one young Christian was talking about "God will provide" when members of this gang started spitting. He put up his umbrella and made his point effectively! On Christian festival occasions, like Christmas and Easter we took our 'open-airs' into the main street, and against the noise of the traffic, the rushing activity of the crowds, and often in the biting cold, we struggled to proclaim. We never knew what seeds we sowed, and maybe this work was in its infancy, but at least I feel that the people of Tunstall knew the Church was there, that it was young and virile, and that it cared.

Bridges were being built from the young Church to the world, from the moment of decision into the new Christian life - and bridges from the Christian to the non-Christian within the group. There is no doubt that the "Helpers" Meeting became the hub of this and all other Group activity. At first I acted entirely independently in selecting from among the young Christians those with leadership potential, whom we came to call Helpers, (we could hardly call them leaders, as this would lead to difficulties with their own peer group). My choice was often haphazard and I often made mistakes, until I came to develop a more certain policy. We came to look for "Helpers" to be firstly Christians with leadership potential, and then members of Tunstall Methodist Church. When the time came for new appointments, either through natural growth or through loss of helpers who went to College or University, I began to ask the current Helpers to talk confidentially about those within their own groups whom they thought were suitable, and about their strengths and weaknesses. I listened to the comments and then went away and prayed, before I made up my own mind. Each Helper had a pastoral responsibility for the discussion group he led, bringing them to Christ or helping them with any particular problems. He needed to become a real trusted friend of others in his group, and to set an example in the Christian life (which we all fail to do from time to time). He took some responsibility for general organisation, and fed ideas in and out of the Helpers meeting. It was a great training for young people, but Helpers were not chosen on the basis of what was good for them, but rather on what was good for the group. The Helpers meeting was once a month, and it planned the programme for the next month. Never without impassioned discussion, it was a fairly informal meeting, looked forward to, and always finishing with open prayer.

And once a year we held a Helpers' Conference, a weekend away to plan the new session together. One such was at Blaithwaite House in Cumberland, where a barn had a false floor put in, and dormitory bedrooms were below, while a lounge and long kitchen range were above. Our prayers were directed and purposeful: "Lord, help us to know what is your will and have the grace to do it.." "Bring...... to Christ, Lord." "Help......with this problem and teach us how we should act with her." "Guide our choice of subjects for the new session, and help us to meet individual needs." We worked and planned hard, and sitting in the oak beamed room in a circle of armchairs we had the sense of God's guiding hand as we sang, "And didst thou cast our lot in this same age and place, and hast together brought to see each other's face." We may have peeled and eaten too many carrots, we may have laughed ourselves silly playing 'Donkey' on the table tennis table, we may have teased and leg-pulled one another through a sunny country stroll, but we were God's people and this was His work to which we had been called. And each new year beckoned with the promise of His grace.

Chapter 13
GUN END HOUSE

Somewhere between Danebridge and Wincle in Derbyshire, at the foot of Gun Hill, there stood a tiny Methodist Chapel. It was closed and in disrepair when we first saw it, its green stone walls peered through the leafy foliage of unpruned tall trees, on the corner of a sharp left hand bend. Surrounded by farm land and fields, its paths were overgrown with thick bushes, and its outside chemical toilet was a masterpiece of country neglect. Inside, there was room for sixty people on long brown forms; it had a tiny pulpit and pedal organ; the walls were damp and glistening, the back one crowned with the words "We worship the crucified Christ" and there was a blackened boiler room, where an underground stream ran in to the fabric of the building. Closed only a few months before it came to our attention, its congregation, which had lovingly maintained worship and Sunday School over many years, were transferred to the chapel at Danebridge.

We were looking for just such a chapel. Some of the first young Christians wanted a practical outlet for their faith, and one Sunday night we had debated beginning a coffee bar in town versus building a retreat centre in the country for deprived children and others. The latter won, and we travelled the local countryside (as far as Wales!) looking for the right place. Somehow we knew when we went inside Gun End Chapel that we had found it.

It was gloomy and damp, but its furniture, well preserved, had the character of nineteenth century Methodism, and a hymn on the pedal organ produced the atmosphere. The trustees were young and keen. When we met with them they responded warmly to the idea of their chapel being used in a continuing Christian way. Not so all the village. A protest meeting was held at the local primary school. Some of the locals did not fancy the idea of townie peace with transistors and motorbikes, and littering the countryside and leaving gates open in typical townie fashion. We went to one of their meetings to try to placate them, but some of them were to remain lively opposition during the five years it took to turn the premises into a habitable Conference Centre. Had we known how long it would take, how much sweat. And Labour and money, how many frustrations and delays, I am sure we would never have started. But we jumped in with both wet innocent feet, agreed on a peppercorn rent, and began application to the Peak Planning Board for change of use. The Board is rightly careful to preserve its countryside, and the agreement we achieved was hedged with limitations and instructions, the most important of which was the need to acquire adjoining land to take any cars off the road. We managed to lease a piece of adjoining land, and laid a temporary car park, surrounded by the requisite bushes and trees. And then we began work on the ground, hacking our way through the undergrowth, touching no trees which were under preservation order, digging and laying concrete paths down the sides of the chapel, laying the beginning of lawns and planting roses.

But what we needed most was money. Over the five years we raised around five thousand pounds by plays and concerts, garden parties, coffee mornings and sponsored walks. One such walk was a distance of twenty three miles, along windy bumpy roads to Gun End and back. Eighty of us walked, Mr. Thompson among them, and I well remember the crippling last lap walking on the sides of the feet, seized up from the hips down, wondering what could possibly have inspired such madness. But it was the heyday of such walks, and what is more, we all enjoyed it. We had decided that we would spend no money if we did not have it, and it was the slow rate at which we raised it which caused the job to take so long. Young people often criticise the Church because, among other things, it always seems to be 'after your money' so we determined that money raising would always play little more than a minor role in our activities, and we always sought to swamp our programme with what was a directly evangelical purpose. So it came to be that Gun End chapel, Gun End House, as we named it, was to be used in the future only for Conferences and retreats that were Christ centred with Christian leaders who would design their own programme, whether it be for deprived children or Group members, or groups and fellowships from other places, so that the spirit of Christ could play His central role.

To that end we worked. The outer brickwork had crumbled and decayed with the years and had to be replaced; the floor had dry rot which had to be cut out, and the new and remaining old boards creosoted from below; the damp walls demanded new roof tiles and cleaning out the cavity ventilation, and outer protection. We found a farmer who enjoyed destroying things, including the chimney and the toilet. Stairs were put down to the boiler room, and an R.S.J. marked the beginnings of a bedroom floor. We had employed an architect whose officially approved designs included two bedrooms covering half the main building, a large lounge to seat thirty five, a kitchen, two toilets and two showers and washing areas. Keith worked during his University holidays as labourer for the man who was putting up the partition walls. We stripped the plaster, and laid new floor-boards around. The thick brick had to be knocked out at the pulpit end so that new windows could be put in. Parties of young people went out nearly every Saturday for many months at a time to clean and paint, scrub and polish. We learned a lot as we went along - how to tongue and groove, the techniques of tiling, painting and plastering, and cementing. But we learned fellowship and teamwork most. Many an autumn Saturday passed surrounded by bare boards and brick walls, sitting on old upright chairs eating butties and drinking cups of hot coffee, congratulating ourselves on tiny jobs completed, sometimes to be undone because they were done too early or done wrong. One Easter we went on a hike through wretched weather and ended up, thirty of us, sitting on the floor of Gun End singing hymns and drinking soup kindly provided by John and Dorothy Kay, two of the trustees from Bent Farm, while Melvyn's brother, Keith and I astonished the mobile fish and chippy people with an order for thirty. We saved Greenshield stamps for twenty five chairs, and people donated carpet tiles for the lounge. The Army gave us bunk beds, and furniture came from the Christian folk of the Potteries. We had a new wiring system, and hired plasterers for the entire building; then we painted the lounge in cream and blue, and tiled the kitchen and toilet areas. The sink units and plumbing were a hefty bill, as was the septic tank. But it was a great day when we switched the water on - it was then that we knew we were really in business!

Somehow the chapel never lost its atmosphere. It became like a home, turquoise carpet and doors, shiny teak open staircase, black beamed, large hanging light globes and dainty side lights, big fridge and cooker, and stainless steel sink, with two stained glass windows preserving the 'chapel' image, it had a hushed holiness which was both warm and gripping. Of course it remained unfinished for years. It needed a fire escape before anyone could stay the night, and there were hundreds of tiny items missing which every householder will know make up the perfect home. But it was opened and well used for ten years. We invited all those who had contributed, to a short dedication service and tour one Saturday in 1974. They came in convoys, as they would not all fit in at one worship, and then came together for a thanksgiving service in Tunstall on the following Saturday evening. And since that day the building came into increasingly regular use. Those who erected her in love, and in the spirit of the great Primitive Methodist revival, must have smiled down as lusty young voices filled the old premises made new with the praise of God.

Chapter 14
A PROPHET IS NOT WITHOUT HONOUR

It's easy when looking back to see only the golden days. But some of them were distinctly dirty. Opposition is an integral part of Christian growth, and our opponents were so varied, and represented so many shades of opinion that I often wondered what opinion there was left for us ourselves to hold! It was amazing how many Christians, ministerial and lay, were totally unwilling to accept that they had actually found an example of God at work, and sought desperately to find some other explanation. "What is the sociological reason for this upsurge in interest?" We were often asked "Are you middle class, or is the identification with the peer group the strength?" "They're all the same sort of people; it must be the influence of one man over them all; they're brainwashed." "They're all nice religious types – but they'll grow out of it." And from parents, the very usual in response to professions of conversion, "It's nice that you're interested in the Church, but don't get too involved, will you dear?" Or the more alarmed, in response to the call of God to a Christian vocation, "You'll turn into a religious fanatic if you're not careful." It was frustrating hearing all these comments second-hand (for I never met them face to face for many years), and wanting to be able to answer them one by one, but never having the chance. But I came to know that the answer to each lies in the continuous holy progression of the stable committed Christian life. The young man of intelligence who hands in his notice to his employer so that he may enter the Christian ministry; the young Christian married couple who bring a child into the world and raise him in the traditional style of a loving committed Christian home; the young person in the midst of suffering and tragedy, who shown his elders how to cope because of his committed Christian faith which produces hope out of despair. These and the years are the answer.

The truth is that this was not my work, or the work of a group, it was the work of God, and if it was truly the work of God, then nothing would destroy it. Nor were they all 'nice religious people'. They came from every background, and the religious influence was probably the weakest in our permissive age. We had our struggles with drugs and devils, with thefts and threatened suicides, with sexual problems and personality disorders. We had Pentecostals and charismatics, Catholics and Baptists, all pressing their own particular theological position, but we found a real unity in the spirit of Christ which made denominational barriers irrelevant, though often valuable in the representation of the rich wealth of Christian experience. We put up with 'my own brand of

Christianity' peddlers, tongues and stickers, tracts and Jesus chants. Not that any of these was either completely good or completely bad. From each we learned; from each we drew new experience, and adjusted our thought and practice to try to take account of what God was saying through them.

Not everyone who first made a decision for Jesus has remained faithful. Many a time we ached and prayed for those we loved who seemed temporarily bewildered by the pressure of twentieth century living. And we often had age old argument about whether once saved is always saved. Somehow I believe that the seed once sown will reap its harvest in its own time. I profoundly hope so.

So despite the drawbacks, numbers grew in the group and in the groups and societies which felt the influence of those who came from it. We even saw adults affected and converted, or searching for the truth. May that continue. For every 'Jim' and 'Doris' (the Group words for male and female!) can know the love of Christ.

In the autumn of 1974 we took our courage in both hands yet again, and divided the group. All those over eighteen were put in house groups, and the students into student groups. We were left with fifty or sixty members of the Youth Group proper. We felt it was so easy for Sunday night to become a social occasion for those who had long been members, when we wanted to continually bring into the fold new faces ready to discover afresh the riches of Christ. It was like going back to Square One; only this time there were three Squares, each related to the other, each with its own particular needs, and each struggling to find its role in the new situation.

Chapter 15

COVENANT CUPBOARD

It is surprising how the basic bread and butter of the Group changed little in the next twenty years, though its circumstances did. Sunday meetings have continued in full flow for the whole of that period - we have never closed, even when the majority of the members have been away on a Group holiday. Helpers have come and gone into Christian service in the wider world, but the Helpers meeting has continued to plan its programme in the same relaxed, humorous, informal but efficient style on a more or less monthly basis. I remember that at an early annual Helpers' conference at Gun End, one Helper was horrified by the amount of her time she would be giving to Group events, and the speed with which this seemed to organise away the year, but in general Helpers have been remarkably loyal and committed in the face of a demanding programme, and much of the success of the work must be laid at their door. In September 1977, we celebrated our tenth birthday with conference, celebration and buffet. Old friends returned and delighted in being together. Claud Thompson's wife Edith, cut the cake, and Melvyn bought a communion chalice and plate which has been in use at conferences and small group meetings ever since.

A host of Greek words marked various new ventures: Didache, for regular in-depth Bible studies on week day nights, Diakonia, for the continuing programme of social concern, particularly amongst deprived children and the elderly, Soteria, for Rob's Gospel Group, which included some outstanding musicians, and travelled the country with its evangelistic message, and Koinonia, for fellowship conferences and groups which flowered particularly in the early 80's. Diakonia is still very active, and its wide ranging programme has its roots in that first deprived children's holiday to the Lake District when two leaders and ten children never allowed the torrential rain to dampen their spirits.

Musical plays and concerts have always continued to be presented. There have been many highlights. Rob and I continued to write, though some of the early plays have undergone serious revision, and been re-presented in new venues, local and national. 'Any Other Name' particularly has stood the test of time, recently finding the light of day again in 1996, in a school hall, as the first production of a relatively new church plant. New plays in the '70's included 'Midsummer Swallow' and Straws in the Wind', and that era also saw productions of our own versions of 'Joseph' and 'Godspell', with their Christian content enlarged and emphasised. This was the period when new music was coming into the Church. 'Together', a really committed and energetic group of young women in flowing robes presented really worshipful music and dance for morning and evening services, and were much in demand. O.C.M. (Original Christian Music) was a forerunner of modern day praise groups, and set very high standards for the writing and performance of Christian music.

Conferences and holidays grew in popularity and numbers. St. Andrews remained a popular holiday venue, with its University, golf course and beach. The Pancake House was a major attraction, but those who went North of the Border would probably best remember the Youth Centre attached to the Baptist church where we met for epilogues, and where the Baptist minister, Rev. Tait, enjoined us, in Scottish twang, to 'Press on!' Those words have been prophetically important at many stages in the Group's life.

In the 70's over 200 young people were involved with the life of the Group, and the majority of these attended regularly on Sunday nights. A series of change of venues had taken place as the Methodist churches in Tunstall had come under compulsory purchase, and various congregations had united in preparation for a new building with a new central witness. These changes had only increased the growth of the Group. At a Faith supper on the evening of Church Harvest in the early 70's over 220 young people brought an absolutely huge and varied buffet to eat together, and celebrated their fellowship in Christ with enthusiasm and reverence. But within a very short time difficulties in the life of the Church seemed to affect numbers and commitment. Many of the original members had long since left to serve Christ elsewhere, some into the ministry, but a core of originals, now adult and some with young families, still directed the work. Many of the young people stopped coming, some claimed to have 'lost their faith' (did they therefore ever have hold of it properly?), others found different spiritual homes. Sunday night attendances plummeted to the early 40's and it became difficult in the new church premises where the home we were given was inappropriate, and the space for storage insufficient, to maintain these numbers. This was a real time of testing. Though there were still conversions, some of them long term significant, there was a loss of morale, and clashes and disagreements within the Church affected the old atmosphere of love. I became seriously concerned when I realised the state the adult leaders had reached in their own personal pilgrimage. We began to search round actively to find an outside source of help and inspiration, and were to see the Lord's hand clearly at work in directing us to and through that source.

We saw a week-end conference advertised to take place at the Hayes Conference Centre, Swanwick, from 7 to 9 October, 1977, and a small group of us decided to attend. We did not know anything about its organisers, the Fountain Trust, an interdenominational group seeking to encourage the spiritual renewal of life within the church, and part of the charismatic movement. We were a little late arriving, and as we crossed the main hall the spiritual joy and peace of a congregation singing modern songs from 'Sound of Living Waters' hit us with considerable force. There was a real refreshment in the music alone. The whole conference opened our eyes to that very significant area of the faith overlooked and neglected by ourselves, as by many other Christians - the activity and power and grace of the living Holy Spirit. By the end of the week-end some of our group had been baptised in the Spirit, and I myself was spoken to in the final service by the Lord, when in silent prayer about the problems we were experiencing back home, I asked two questions of the Lord, and from different parts of the large hall, two people totally unknown to me gave two direct and specific answers to my questions. 'Lord, you are silent in all this mess. Where are you? You haven't spoken' and the answer, ' "I have spoken" says the Lord. "You have seen many come to me. I have not been silent, I have spoken", says the Lord.' 'But what am I to do to change the situation?' and the answer, "You are to wait", says the Lord, "you are to wait for a sign".' Tom Smail, who was leading the meeting, interrupted the prayer time to say, 'Something very significant has just happened to someone in this hall. They should stand and affirm it.' I did not have sufficient courage, and the meeting moved on after a pause in which one other person spoke her thoughts. I remembered to wait for a time, but the pressure of events put the waiting out of my mind till it returned to me some time later in a remarkable way.

We returned home from that weekend with a new spirit (literally!) and a new determination to bring this spiritual renewal into the life of the Group. O.C.M. and Together flowed from this, I think, or at least were very affected by it, but just as significant was our attempt to organise a conference of a similar nature for the Class Meetings at Shallowford House from 2 to 4 June, 1978. We invited Rev. Buchan, Head of R.E. at the Sixth Form College, and a gentle Christian involved in the charismatic movement and touched by the Spirit, to lead some sessions and our final service. As I was setting out the chairs in a circle in the lounge, the words, 'You are to wait for a sign' returned to me with force, and in that meeting through a particular Bible passage, the Lord explained to me the way in which He was using the difficult events in the Church to teach me a personal lesson. As I read the words I was transfixed, and was almost totally unaware of those members who in this meeting received the Spirit through the laying on of hands. All I could do was read the passage over and over again. There was personal growth and renewal for me, and a lesson I must always seek not to ignore. The blessings of this week-end led to the first Prayer and Praise meetings at which we sought to allow the Spirit freedom to move. Meetings of this nature have come and gone over the years. Sometimes we have been tremendously blessed through them, and have discovered the exercise of various gifts of the Spirit, but often we have had to bring them to an end when they have become formalised and dry. They have often been attended by the curious and onlookers, as well as those who are genuinely open to the Spirit, and we have not been successful in dealing with this situation. And perhaps this freedom of the Spirit should be best expressed in the Sunday worship of the Churches to which we have belonged; we still hope for this to happen.

Though many of us found renewed faith through these events, our problems within the Church had not run away. At Easter 1979 we met in Mal's house to discuss what we were to do about them, and decided that if we were to keep the work going we would have to find an alternative home. We sought what the Lord was saying to us through prayer, and eventually felt led to take the Sunday evening meetings to a small Methodist chapel about half a mile away from Tunstall. So on the night of the Church Family Celebration at Tunstall, in pouring rain, we loaded our worldly goods, a large grey filing cupboard full of books and materials, onto a trailer attached to Rob's car, and took it to the little chapel. We had discussed the matter with the Burslem Circuit minister who had pastoral charge, and he welcomed us there. We informed the Group meeting of 35 that this was to be our new home, and like Moses, we went out into the wilderness with what become known as our "covenant" cupboard. It was all very uncertain and traumatic, and still causes me some pain, but its effects were very dramatic. We faced the summer months, when holidays usually depressed numbers, but there was an inflow of members, so that by September we were getting between 60 and 70 regularly on a Sunday night. The small congregation were bemused by this sudden inflow of worshippers, for those of us who were Methodist members sought to give ourselves to the total life of the Church, and in the end several stalwarts in the congregation felt they could not cope with this explosion, and refused at a Church Council to accept our membership. In the meantime, Rev. Dr. Arthur Shaw, Chairman of the District and long time friend of the Group, had sought to encourage us at various meetings to consider finding a home at Burslem Central Methodist Mission, Swan Bank, where the minister, Rev. Brian Kirkpatrick, a gracious and lively evangelical, was willing to welcome us with open arms. At a prayer meeting, one of our number had a word from the Lord, and it was to 'Take this, my church, into this my open house, that you may receive my perfect blessing.' So, on Sunday 29 July, the cupboard was on the move again, and found its new home in this historic old church with one of the oldest Sunday schools in the country, where Arnold Bennett attended, a church whose history was tied up with the story of the Primitive Methodist movement. Its Sunday school rooms, large and meandering, were a historically listed building; its worship centre was modern and light; its congregation were struggling to maintain an effective Christian witness in the heart of one of the Six Towns, and it presented many wonderful opportunities and openings. When one Sunday night in our new home, 35 new Swan Bank members, some young, some adult, and some even older people who had loyally and wonderfully supported us in this transfer, joined with the rest of the congregation in singing the hymn 'All will be well' I strongly felt that this was the promise of God for now.

Chapter 16
THE SWAN BANK GROUP

So our name changed. We became the Swan Bank Group, and we resumed our meetings on Sunday nights in what became known as the Fellowship Room, a long rectangular room in the modern part of the building. By September 1980 we had 100 or more regular attenders, and the spiritual atmosphere returned to its old self. Brian Kirkpatrick really encouraged us by his constant support, his input, and his attempts to involve us in the life of the Church. He was in the process of renovating almost single handed one of the large lower halls of the Sunday School building, and all its upper rooms, and some joined him in this, removing windows, painting and decorating just as in the old Gun End days. We made contributions to the evening worship, though the congregation was well used to the classic Central Hall type worship, and was not yet ready for wholesale change. Nevertheless, we found them welcoming and supportive, and in the three years he was with us, Brian fielded any difficulties or misunderstandings. The Group magazine 'Shake' became the Church magazine, and the Church worship centre itself became the home for some of our musical and dramatic productions like 'Fishers of Men', 'If my People' and later, 'The Greatest Show on Earth'. Some productions went to the Queens Theatre just up the road. Conferences and holidays resumed as normal. We stayed in Plymouth Polytechnic twice and then in Aberdeen. Among remarkable happenings in the 1980's was the musical 'Plucked from the Burning', the story of the life of John Wesley, in which District young people joined, producing several significant conversions amongst them. This was followed by 'Mow Fire' which began with the story of Bourne and Clowes, and looked for the fire of God to return. Extracts from it were presented to the President of the American Methodist Conference and his party in a local hotel, and it was then revisited for the Burslem Methodist Conference in 1986. In 1988, the musical 'Switchblade', the story of Nicky Cruz was taken for two nights to the theatre in the round, a really appropriate venue. The New Victoria Theatre was packed out on both evenings, and the play was very effective. There were many other productions; perhaps the most significant thing to say about them all is they succeeded in bringing people who had little or no previous contact with the Church into a personal relationship with Jesus, as many of them still attest. They were often hard work, and one or two of them nearly drove the producer to distraction, especially where less loyal members failed to turn up for rehearsal or dropped out altogether! But then, that's par for the course. We all got particular joy from joining in the national work of the Methodist evangelist Rob Frost whenever he brought his team to the area. In March 1983 the Group provided the whole of the backing choir (120 of them!) for 'Daybreak' in the Kings Hall, Stoke, also packed for the occasion. Another memorable occasion was 'Visions' at Birmingham's National Exhibition Centre in 1984, when we prepared and performed one of the scenes, looking like ants in that mighty arena. These were happy, settled years, of good fruit, though inevitably they had their problems.

Brian Kirkpatrick was succeeded after three years by John Hibberts. He and his wife Val are both originally from North Staffordshire and understand the delicacy and sensitivity of the people (like the china product they produce, as Brian Kirkpatrick once put it!) because they feel it themselves. They are both keen evangelical Christians, but, despite that, they would both testify that the early years of adjusting to the peculiar nature of the Group, and drawing together the Group and the Church were very painful. John was to be particularly successful in drawing the young adults in successive waves into the full life of the Church, a happening Brian had begun but had not had time to complete, but one that I had always longed for. At first at Swan Bank it was difficult to deal with the young adults, who had outlived the Group programme, and were uneasy in the life of the Church. We tried various experiments, including Sunday night House Groups for them, which had some good positive results because of their keen and able leaders, and then a Bridging Group, which was supposed to look at issues in more depth, and to bridge the gap between Group and Church. This was not completely successful; maybe I didn't think it through sufficiently, or maybe we were really just biding time while the Church changed. And change it certainly did! The modern Church music of the Chris Bowater's and Graham Kendrick's of the '80's gave the opportunities for gifted musicians to form increasing numbers of praise bands, worship became more varied and informal, the OHP found its ever more prominent place, and drama and dance were widely used. John was able to respond to the ideas of the young people, involve them in worship, and to gently lead the more traditional congregation to appreciate the benefit of what was proposed. The programme of the Church expanded massively too, and within its broad arms many young adults found opportunity for service. The Group has produced very many ministers and local preachers. As far as the latter are concerned, this has significantly affected the Burslem Mission Circuit, until comparatively recently a two church circuit. Currently there are thirty one preachers, twenty of whom come from the Group, and many of them offer themselves more widely to the surrounding circuits as opportunities for preaching in one's home base are rather limited

Over a period of years the older members of the Group transferred from evening to morning worship with their young families, and so morning worship has grown and changed, becoming larger than the evening service, and spawning an earlier quieter service, which at time of writing is in its early stages. Parents, families and friends have found their place within this warm and welcoming fellowship, as have very many others drawn in by John Hibberts' personal evangelism, winning personality and tireless work. So the Group has been able to cease being a Church of its own, but has grown into the life of the whole community of God's people.

The group held its twenty first birthday celebrations in 1988. The evening celebration on 19 March was a time of nostalgia and praise. As the birthday brochure says 'Through all those years its aim has always been to lead people into a personal relationship with Jesus Christ as their Lord and Saviour, and to help them grow as Christians' and we saw evidences of that all around us, and we praised the Lord for it! But the weekend conference at Swanwick was even more powerful. We were joined by so many of those who had found their way through the Group, and were now serving Christ elsewhere. There was a warmth of love and fellowship, a looking forward in excitement and anticipation, a sense of repentance and beginning again amongst all the teenagers, younger and older families. When the children of Group members joined us to express their own faith and commitment in the Sunday morning worship, I think Heaven really smiled.

Chapter 17
MOVING ON

Gun End has passed from us. After ten years of hosting conferences and courses, the little chapel was returned to its circuit, and was eventually sold to become the home of a Christian and Methodist family, who have preserved all its features. It had done its job well, but it was at a distance from Stoke, was difficult to oversee in the winter, and in any case it was time to move on. It typifies the truth that in expressing the life of the Kingdom in this impermanent world, some things are everlasting and some are bound to change. This chapter is about the most significant of those changes, some of which have far wider and larger significance than the Group itself.

Over the years we gathered a large amount of original musical and dramatic material which should have been a resource for the wider church. It was difficult to get any of it published, and so Geoff Bond and I came up with the idea that we should have a resource centre ourselves where others could come to borrow material. Geoff had been a member of the Group since the Tunstall days, and as a local preacher, worship leader, actor and singer, was very interested in producing for a wider audience what was good in what we had produced. He and I went to seek Brian Kirkpatrick while he was still with us to investigate whether there was a possibility of using a church room. Brian was very sympathetic, but it was difficult to allocate a room solely for that purpose, so I began to look around elsewhere. After much looking at vacant premises, I came across a set of first floor rooms over Barclay's Bank in Burslem, Geoff and I and three other friends and Group stalwarts agreed together to cover the cost of a lease over a period of years, and so the "Saltbox" was born. There used to be a chapel in Burslem known locally as the Saltbox because of the quality of life of its members - they were salt to the world! That seemed to be a name worth preserving!

We began to advertise in Christian magazines, purchased an answering machine, and two or three times a week after work I called in to answer the mail and listen to the messages. Slowly interest began to grow, and we found the premises very useful when the church was oversubscribed. Eventually we were able to advertise for an employee on a small, sacrificial salary, and Paul Truby joined us. The Saltbox has its own exciting story to tell, which no doubt will one day be written. Suffice to say, small beginnings have produced a work which is now acting as an encouragement and support to all denominations in North Staffordshire, drawing them together in love and united witness, making a known impact on the secular world, and moving towards a future which should be very significant in the life of the city. I'm so glad the Lord is using those original, simple, but well meant ideas in such a useful way to His glory.

In 1990 I felt it was time to move on personally. I passed through a time when the Helpers of that generation and I did not see eye to eye, and I felt discouraged. I sought to be faithful, and was particularly strongly supported by Rob Phillips in leading the Group through several years. But I was tired, and though I still had much to give, I needed a rest. So, after a sabbatical to ensure that the Group would still go on faithfully if I departed - no one is indispensable - I passed the leadership over to Lloyd Cooke.

Lloyd had found Christ at the end of an epilogue one Sunday night at the Group, was a good friend, had become the Director of Saltbox, and had many of the qualities necessary in a youth leader, one of the key ones being tireless commitment. And in 1997 the Group is still there, although the leadership has changed again!

The programme continues in much the same way. There have been experiments, but the tried formula still seems best for 1990's young people. I am delighted to say that young people still continue to be won for Christ, young leaders are being grown up, and the interests and energies of many still centre round Jesus Christ. Fifty to sixty young people still meet each Sunday, with bigger events drawing over a hundred. Long may it continue.

For myself, at the end of 1990 I joined my brother Phil, the visionary for this outreach, and some other Swan Bank members in going to plant a church on the Birches Head estate in the Hall of the local High School. It has grown and developed over a six year period, and Birches Head Christian Fellowship has become the third church of the Burslem Mission Circuit. I have many responsibilities there, not least leading the Youth Group! We began with three or four people in a member's house. We have grown till there are now about thirty five on our books, twenty five of whom attend regularly. We meet in the Pavilion of Northwood Sports Centre on Friday nights at eight. Our young Christians meeting is on Sunday nights (yes, about eight young people have given their lives to Christ). They are gradually finding a place in the life of the church. Will they stick the course? It's certainly too early to say, but I don't think I'm being foolish in believing that they stand in the same succession. A similar programme, a similar approach. Why not try it yourself?

POSTSCRIPT - A MANUAL FOR YOUTH LEADERS

THE PERSONNEL

Let us begin this manual with the 'punters.' Every organisation is into market research in the late twentieth century. I believe that any youth based market research will show you that much of the following is true. There may or may not be a generation gap these days, but there is certainly still a culture gap. In terms of age, it is the post war versus the pre-war generations, and it expresses itself in terms of an attitude to life, a sense of formality or informality, a style of dress, a taste in music, the use of leisure time, and in many other ways. Much of the post war generation is more laid back in its attitude to life than the generations which preceded the Second World War. Many of the former see money in terms of its spending power, relationships in terms of their power to give pleasure, status as largely irrelevant, rights as more significant than responsibilities, and life to be good fun. Informality, colour and fashion really matter, and are means of personal expression, ways of making an impact, of being noticed. 'Dressing up for the occasion' is less important than making everyone feel relaxed, being comfortable, and bringing down the barriers of formality and stiffness that appear to separate people. The impact of modern music and the technological revolution have meant that noise and beat and melody are inter-related, and the growth in advertising has meant that modern music is more widely known and appreciated and understood than is the music of past generations. Despite recessions and the fear of unemployment (and unemployment itself) many of the post war generation have money in their pockets to spend on lively and interesting forms of entertainment; if they save, it is often in the short term, and for a specific purpose. Respect has to be earned; experience and position do not really rate, though knowledge and ability still count for much. Most of all, many of them believe that all people are just people, and that people of all ages and sexes and colours and nationalities are to be treated as though the masks and barriers and divisions which separate one person from another are not there.

CULTURE GAP IN THE CHURCH

One of the problems that many of the established churches of this country have had for the last forty years is that this culture gap is often reflected in the life of the individual church. Many of the pre-war generation who are worshipping regularly are there first because of their faith, but also because they have found the church to be a bastion of changelessness in a disturbing world of continuous change and apparent deterioration. The bewildering changes of the twentieth century can be laid aside for an hour every Sunday to worship in reverence and quietness, using the same forms as have been used for generations past. The beauty of Evensong, the solemnity of the Mass, the predictability of the five hymn sandwich are a security, a safeness, a rock of ages under which to shelter. So when the teens or twenties or thirties wander into church dressed in jeans, chat animatedly to each other before the service begins, prefer the N.I.V. to the A.V., like open prayer and testimony, raise their hands in worship, or clap, are openly scornful of the anthems of the choir, and actually like a praise band leading worship, the gap is strained to breaking point. The security of the older worshipper is undermined, and the two sides find they cannot understand one another's attitudes and behaviour at all. I doubt that this difference of approach to worship can be resolved in any other way than by taking the best of the old, making it communicative in modern day terms, and allowing the rest to slide quietly onto the back burner. Certainly, in an era when worship needs to be increasingly seeker friendly if the message of the church is not to be lost, the culture of the church must match the culture of the world. And here I speak of the medium; the message is eternal. Older people need not fear; the church and the faith will not die - we are just seeking a new pattern of communication to post-Christian Britain. And this communication will be very useful in causing church growth, allowing church planting to be effective, and helping seeker services to reach those outside the faith. It's sad that, because young people are on one side of this culture gap, they are often vilified by church goers for attitudes and behaviour they have largely inherited. Young people are after all just people, like the rest of humanity. This is obvious enough to sound trite, and yet failure to grasp it is the basic problem that many adults have with the young; they speak of them as though they are a race apart, alien beings, who have flown in from nowhere to occupy their particular part of the planet. Words like 'youngsters', 'kids', 'the youth of today', are not just means of identification - they also intend, consciously or unconsciously, alienation. It is really quite amazing how quickly those past the age of twenty five forget that they were ever young, or felt any of the feelings, or had any of the experiences, which belong to those below that age. We can easily find ourselves addressing the teens and twenties differently from the way we address all others. We might be guilty of being condescending, talking down, without meaning to, and so erect barriers. The minister who announces, 'Our young people will sing for you', instead of 'Some of our church members will....' needs to be careful, as do older church members when they say 'We must have something for the young people'. 'You'll understand when you're as old as I am', or 'You don't know what life's like yet' are comments bound to raise the hackles of the most moderate teenager. The culture gap is only crossed when we realise we are all on the same journey of life, and that there is no magic line which you cross to move from 'youngster' to 'grown up'. We have similar fears, hang ups, joys and excitements as one another, and our differences lie not in the sort of people we are, but in the sort of society we are born into and brought up in. The 'them' and 'us' attitude of some church members, youth leaders or ministers, which separates the young from the old, will cause the sort of barriers which lose young people to the church, and denies the very meaning of 'the Body of Christ.' The church is surely the family of God, and elders lead youngers to become elders in their turn. Birth and death are experiences in common, and to cry 'I don't understand young people these days' is to forget the commonness of those experiences which bind us all together in the mystery of life. But young people too are sometimes guilty of inventing that generation gap which never really exists, and can be as arrogant and unfeeling about 'the older generation.' I think they are often led into this by the attitude and behaviour of those older than themselves who have created their world for them. It is still true however that when you are first discovering independence in the freshness of life that you are dismissive of 'wrinklies' whom you think have had their time. A good youth programme will seek to make its members aware of this in themselves, and make efforts to correct it. In any congregation there are usually a few people who relate easily to teens and twenties, even though sometimes they may be considerably older. I have found that this often relates to their own living Christian experience, whose vitality becomes more attractive the older they become, and which draws everyone of every age towards themselves. Our physical bodies may be in decay, but inwardly we are renewed by the power of Christ, and inward renewal allows for no gap across the generations. Our cultures may be different, but our common experience of Him cannot be denied.

OUR POST CHRISTIAN SOCIETY

Most people in this country do not know or understand the Christian gospel. They live for this life, and that is all they know. We live in a bewildered, acquisitive society. There is a sense of insecurity everywhere. We have so many pressures and demands made on us from the rising clamour of many different interests. So the average person lives for today, and seeks to acquire a comfortable and pleasant home, a good car, a reasonably happy family life, and restful or energetic leisure time. Life is constantly under threat, but as has often been observed, death, not sex, is the taboo subject, the very thought of which is pushed into a dark corner. It is this sort of society that our young inherit, and so, to some degree, they are as society makes them. They know Jesus as a hero figure who is reasonably attractive, but the significance of whose life is little appreciated. The Church is seen to be old fashioned, irrelevant, out of date, peculiar. And religious people are largely thought to be fanatics, 'nutters', people whose strange problems cause them to invent a God figure to solve them. I suppose religion is largely outside their experience. There are increasingly lively churches which attract those in their teens and twenties, but most young people have no contact with the building where the faithful meet, few of them went to Sunday School, and even fewer enjoyed it, and the whole image of the Church is archaic and largely rejected. To get a young person into a church for the first time is as difficult as getting a sixty year old past the bouncers into the local night club-there are the same fears, there is the same sense of alienation. That is why a less threatening, more informal, peer group environment needs to be permanently designed as a bridge over which those in their teens and twenties can cross to reach the continuing fellowship of the church of all ages. It is also one of the reasons, though by no means the only one, why the culture patterns of worship need to be changed if the Church is to avoid being a club for the minority.

THE ENTERTAINMENT SCENE

This generation has more free money to spend than many of its predecessors, and many more opportunities for entertainment. Making friends, and finding a partner, are often done within the context of pub and night club, leisure centre and restaurant. We have immensely improved the facilities in this country for those who have money to burn, and evenings and weekends to do it in. Many new entertainment centres are friendly, warm, colourful and lively; they provide opportunities for sports, dancing, food, drink, and pleasure which attract the young in crowds, and, in a competitive age, are always improving. So a young person's desire for activity can be easily filled if he has the money - evenings and weekends can be occupied with a whirl of excitement, and the contrast between this and the world of church is very marked. There is also, of course, much room for temptation. Drugs are easily available; and I don't just mean crack or heroin. All kinds of illegal drugs are reasonably available for those who are streetwise; in fact any secondary school child will tell you where and how to get them. Parties, pubs and clubs are the place for pushers, who are always at the heels of the susceptible. A constant programme of health education against the background of firm laws energetically enforced provides some degree of protection here. But it is not the complete answer. And the legal and socially acceptable drugs, tobacco and alcohol, can be as addictive and destructive; even the most law abiding and moral may have failed to face the consequences of their misuse. There is also openness about sex, and a large degree of promiscuity. Young people are sexually active younger. Many of them believe that the best way to express love and discover if you are really suited is to have sexual intercourse. The fear of Aids, I suspect, may have tempered promiscuity a little, but the condom is mistakenly seen as the complete protection when you want to enjoy yourself. It is difficult for a person in their teens or twenties to come to terms with a biblical concept of morality which frowns on fornication and adultery, two 'old fashioned' words. A faithful and permanent view of marriage is not commonly practised. Adolescence is the age of experiment; bodily urges are strong and demanding. A life long relationship may still develop out of this new relationship culture, but it is as likely that there will be the pain of betrayal, and unwanted children, separation or divorce.

IT'S NATURAL TO BE RELIGIOUS

It's normal to have religious feelings; all human beings have a sense of the numinous which they approach with fear and fascination. So in a country where the established churches no longer have the same hold on a large proportion of the population, there is still a search for religious answers. Maybe that is why some young people fall foul of the occult. Ouija boards, spiritualism, seances, astrology and witchcraft - all these have their followers. They are all in the end negative and destructive, and any form of dabbling might lead from easy pastures into a fearful, dark world, from which it is difficult to escape without the power of Jesus. So sometimes the youth leader will find among the young hidden hurts and fears and terrible bondage to those secret things which allow the power of the enemy to range free in their lives, and it is supernatural power from the God of Jesus Christ alone which will bring healing and release.

REJECTION OF AUTHORITY

Many young people do not take easily to authority. The school, the police, the courts, the boss, the church, the parents - they are not easily accepted, nor, it seems, have they ever been. Many of the young grow up by arguing with and opposing them, especially where that authority has not been exercised over them with the proper balance of firmness and love which produces maturity. In an age when authority often does not know its own mind, and behaves in ways which cause total loss of respect, the young are impatient to sweep aside all authority above them, until they themselves are thrust into the role of authority figures. It is, then, often wearying to occupy an authority role, and 'to stand firm against a sea of troubles, and by opposing end them.' But young people eventually discover how tiring it can be to occupy an authority position yourself, believing you have discovered at much personal pain and cost what the received wisdom of the ages is - particularly in Christian terms - and then to find that you cannot persuade the next generation down that this wisdom is right for them too. Each generation needs to find its own way. The key is how to pass on that wisdom without widening the culture gap, or causing alienation.

THE LOVE OF JESUS

It is difficult to determine what is the deepest drive of each of our lives, but one of the strongest motivations is the desire to be loved. In our relationships, at work, at home, in our leisure time, we all seek the approval and affection of others. Our problems multiply when we feel we are rejected or ignored. And imagining or discovering that rejection can be the source of brokenness and illness. The young, like all of us, often experiment with ways of gaining other people's attention and approval. For them, dress and fashion, moral and social behaviour, the use of work and leisure, all are adapted to their conscious or subconscious drive. It takes most people a long time to discover that it is more fulfilling to love than it is to be loved. It is part of the youth leader's task to motivate young people into offering love. If he is fortunate or very able, he may persuade some among his members that love which demands no return is the highest that any human being can achieve. Such love in action is moving and attractive. It is difficult to offer. But there are those who achieve it, both the great and the good who are known for offering their lives selflessly in the service of others, and those from the local community who in their ordinary, everyday lives offer those extremes of sacrificial love in their relationships with their family and friends. Such examples are inspirational, and awaken idealism in the young, and the best of them is the example of Jesus. Here was a man who gave Himself in totally self sacrificing love to the point of death on a cross for the sake of humanity, and His life still stands above any other life as a supreme example of what it means to love God with all your heart and soul and mind and strength, and to love your neighbour as you do yourself. When His life is revealed in all its purity and holiness, then young people are bound to warm to Jesus. The personality of the man, and the power He has to change lives, transfixes young people; it is as though He leaps to life when they read the Bible. Put them within reach of the gospel, and a revolution is worked which is purely of God. It is one of the modern tragedies of the Church that we have so often failed to allow the carpenter from Nazareth to speak to the young on His own terms. I have seen young people come to faith merely by reading about Him, and I am convinced that if we will only have the courage to speak directly of His love in our youth groups each week, we shall again turn the world upside down.

THE PROGRAMME

A weekly meeting of a Christian Youth Group should normally last at most two hours in formal session. Topics need to be varied and stimulating; it is possible to look at an individual topic from various aspects and different angles but precisely the same material cannot be repeated within a five or six year span. During the course of the year there are various events and celebrations which will naturally lead to particular topics, but many evenings will be specially designed by the Youth Leader and his team. The approach too will be very varied. I have found from experience that there are certain ways of approaching a topic which are more helpful than others. Amongst, these, the most commonly used is a programme of an opening introduction, discussion groups and epilogue, and it is with the inestimable value of discussion groups that I begin.

DISCUSSION GROUPS

Every youth group, no matter how small, should allow time for discussion. This opportunity for communication and sharing should be made available to members at least two meetings out of every four. If you begin your youth group with four or five members, they will make up your first discussion group. A good size for a reasonable discussion group however, is about twelve people, and from experience it is best to keep the same people together over a fairly long period. Each group needs two discussion leaders if possible; they can help one another, and one of them can also play devil's advocate. The discussion group leaders' roles are very important; they need to get to know the members of their group well and to be open and welcoming towards new members. They begin each group by introducing by Christian name those who are not known to any other in the Group. I include here the hints we have issued to those who lead discussion groups, with thanks to whoever first wrote them:

Before discussion

(1) Pray - about your group, your fellow discussion group leader, the next discussion time.
(2) Prepare - by thinking around the subject, finding out (if you are somewhat ignorant on the subject concerned); by talking with your fellow discussion group leader about the way you will guide the discussion and who will start it.
(3) Know - where you mean to end up. It is not necessary to know exactly what each stage of the discussion will be, but you must know where it is going, and how to get it there. Because the aim is to win

others for Christ, the end of the discussion will be the moment to further that aim.

At the beginning

1. Seating is important. Make sure you can see everyone and that everyone else can see everyone. Move out physical barriers like tables and pianos!
2. Encourage the atmosphere of friendliness by chatting to people as you/they enter the room. Do not sit next to your fellow discussion group leader, nor in the same spot every week.
3. Introduce new people to the others and make sure you know every one's name.
4. Talk together about any matters relating to your group. This helps new people find their feet, brings the group together as a unit and sets the atmosphere for discussion.
5. Don't be afraid to laugh or make a fool of yourself: laughter breaks down barriers but - enough is enough.
6. Most important point - begin where the group are - not where you are. That means at the level that the youngest - non-Christian - newcomer can appreciate. So the first question will most likely not be the one decided on at the discussion group leaders' meeting, but one that will be a gentle introduction to that, from the experience of your group.
7. A useful beginning is to ask each member of the group to state his opinion on a certain matter that will relate to everyone there. Then the discussion can go on from there. This approach may also be used at a later point in the discussion. Remember that the question must be a general one, relating to everyone's experience. The good thing about this is you can all say something without too much embarrassment.
8. Never use notes; it is a bit off-putting. Know your questions.

During discussion

1. Never ask a question and then answer it. If no-one answers, either ask another question which is easier to understand, or wait and allow your fellow discussion group leader to come to the rescue.
2. Do not dominate the discussion or allow anyone else to dominate it.
3. Occasionally call on silent Christians to speak. They may not be grateful at the time but they usually are later. Do not call on new people or non-Christians.
4. Do not be afraid of silence. It takes some people minutes to find the courage to speak, even in your group!

5. Keep the discussion at the level at which every person is able to understand. Do not let the Christians make it "theological".
6. Good standby questions especially for theological Christians, are "why" and "would you explain what that means?".
7. If the discussion is 90% silence, go back to "at the beginning", point 6.
8. If the discussion wanders away from the topic on to something which would not fulfil the aim of the group, bring it back smartly.
9. If the discussion wanders away from the topic on to something that could fulfil the aim of the group and is causing lively interest, allow it to continue. You will know if it is important to people there.

   Remember that the needs of the folk in your group are far more important than the questions decided at the discussion group leaders' meeting. The questions are only a guide to an end.
10. Do not get lost or too involved personally in the discussion or you will cease to lead it. Always have in your mind the aim of that discussion and not the arguments of the moment.

After discussion

1. Get to know some of your group, especially new members, during refreshments.
2. It may be necessary to chat to one or two of the Christians to remind or tell them of their role in the group, which is to give and not to get.
3. Talk to anyone who needs particular help.
4. Plan activities in which the group can be involved together and so get to know one another e.g. socials, outings etc.
5. Meet your fellow discussion group leader and talk over the discussion and your group in general.
6. Your role as a discussion group leader involves being a Pastor too. Follow-up absences, and show love to those in your care. A list of name and addresses is invaluable.
7. Pray for conversions, for strength, for God's will to be done through you and your group.

These notes indicate that discussion group leaders need to meet together regularly (say once a month) in order to plan their discussions, even if there is only one discussion group, and therefore only two leaders. In order to be able to do this, the material to be discussed each week needs to be known, the leader of each evening should have planned questions he wishes to be discussed, and the leaders need to talk about what answers they would be expecting to hear. I have found it to be helpful at the end of each discussion group for one or other leader to summarise very briefly what has been achieved during the course of the discussion. You may also have noted that after our epilogue we have in the past had some form of refreshments together which provides opportunity for social interaction - it is at this time that some of the difficulties and needs of particular people can be sorted out. So - each of these discussion evenings begins with a short ten to twenty minute introduction and ends with a ten minute epilogue, followed by a social time. Those who lead each evening need to have good communication skills, and discussion group leaders need to have been carefully chosen. Epilogues need to be taken sometimes by leaders and sometimes by members, and a song, a prayer and a short word seem to be sufficient to complete the evening.

These discussion evenings are the basic meat of your Youth Group meetings. A large amount of suitable topic material for Youth Groups is now available nationally, and can be obtained through your local Christian book shop. You may of course prefer to prepare your own topics, biblical, theological, topical, controversial.

Such evenings will be interspersed with rather more varied meetings, ideas for which are included later. One discussion group requires only one meeting room, but as your Youth Group grows you will need to acquire additional rooms for your groups to meet in. Your discussion group leaders may be members of their peer group, but should have real and lively Christian experience, and some degree of development and maturity in the Christian life, as well as potential leadership skills. A person who is very quiet and finds communication very difficult will not make an ideal leader, but such people do grow and develop over a period of years, and it is important to note the progress being made by each member of your group so that all skills may be used. Those who are appointed as discussion group leaders may also have a wider role in the general planning of the weekly activities of your group, but it is also possible to have a different group of people responsible for general planning so that more are involved in leadership responsibility. As well as at least one ongoing activity of social concern, I have found it necessary for the group to interact socially during the week on at least five occasions in a year. We have regularly planned one weekend conference away around the Christmas period, and often a summer holiday of a week or two weeks. It is also necessary for new Christians to have opportunities to express their faith through preaching and evangelism, music, drama, and open air and street witness. The Christian members of the Group will need regular fellowship meetings at least fortnightly when they can learn together about the new faith they have discovered. Putting into operation such a large programme demands a great deal of time and planning, and the involvement of other leaders within a leaders' meeting is absolutely necessary for the Youth Leader of a largish group to survive. You cannot do everything;

hopefully as the programme grows so those who are able to assist in its planning and performance will also grow.

The aim of your programme is to win young people to a clear commitment to Jesus Christ, to help them grow into His Church and into the complete Christian life. This means that much of the programme is about learning, growing and understanding, but occasionally there have to be those times when the challenge of the faith is clearly presented, and an opportunity for response is given. This might be during a particular evening activity; we have commonly offered the Church and its communion rail as a place where the young people who wish to make a commitment to Jesus Christ should go to pray. It might be in one to one conversation, and through prayer, or it might be by taking young people to those concerts, conferences, celebrations and festivals where the opportunity to respond is given. These opportunities need to be carefully prayed over and planned. The leaders need to spiritually discern what is happening within the group and how far individuals have travelled along the road towards faith, so that they may be helped at the right time and in the right place to make the right commitment. There also needs to be a degree of follow-up should a young person make such a commitment to Christ. I believe it is necessary for a person to receive careful counselling immediately following such a decision. We have regularly adopted the six point plan for growth - that is to encourage the convert to pray regularly, to read the Bible regularly (with useful Bible Study notes), to attend Worship regularly, to receive regular Fellowship, to Witness regularly (beginning with members of their own family), and realise that their Faith does not depend upon their feelings - they may at the time of their commitment feel very close to God and very excited, but the time will come when life is hard and problems arise and God seems far away - at such times they should rely on their faith and not on their feelings, and remember the commitment they first made, and they will come through their difficulties. After counselling, the young person should be helped and encouraged into the right sort of Church worship, the proper place for fellowship, and should continue with the Christian friendship he or she has discovered through the group.

A few words about the introduction and the epilogue. An introduction might consist of a straight talk, a short film, a piece of mime or drama, a film strip, a song with guitar, a video, a reading from the newspaper, in fact anything which catches attention; and the introductions will be as varied as possible. Most young people enjoy a short time of worship, and it is important for the group to invest in a good song book and encourage the musical skills of the membership. If a small Praise Band can arise from your members, it can perform a most useful function. There is always time too for new songs. We have found it valuable to have visiting speakers no more than once or twice a year, as, although their ideas are refreshing and stimulating, they are not aware of how to pitch their talk at the right level for the present attitudes of the young people they are talking to, and do not know what has previously been looked at or what is to be looked at shortly.

Those who are experienced in taking epilogues should be given careful guidance and help. Young people are often embarrassed to speak to their peers about their faith, and are inclined to begin an epilogue with a word of apology, usually suggesting that they did not have sufficient time to prepare for the epilogue or that they were diverted from their task. They need to be told to be bold and direct, to be personal and simple, to trust in the Lord as they do their planning and presentation, and never to apologise for what they are offering.

MEETINGS WHICH DO NOT INVOLVE DISCUSSION

Be inventive! The possibilities are very varied. Here are a few suggestions:

1. A song and testimony evening - This consists of carefully chosen Christian songs as a framework within which various leaders and members share testimony about how they came to, or how they now live, their faith. It seems to have added significance if linked to Christmas, Easter or Whitsuntide, and might end with an opportunity for faith response.

2. The writing, preparation, and presentation of Christian drama by different small groups. Can it all be done in one evening? Yes, it can! Young people are very inventive, and can produce humorous, moving or pointed drama, if directed by a suitable theme.

3. At the beginning of the New Year it is a time for looking back, and looking forward. Members share their thoughts, memories and expectations.

4. Harvest - Take out the harvest produce to homes suggested and pre-warned by the Church. A practical exercise in social skills and sharing.

5. Plan together a practical way of helping others. Many good organisations, such as that run by Oasis, now provide excellent material and good suggestions for young people. It is important for members to look at their own community and the wider world with Christian compassion, and to meet that by being actively involved.

6. Ask your minister if the young people can help lead a Youth Service in the Church, and plan such a celebration to involve all your members. Use an evening for rehearsal.

7. A Brains Trust, with a mixture of members and leaders on the panel. Give your discussion group(s) ten minutes to come up with

lively and demanding questions on a Christian theme, and then allow contributions from the floor.

8. We have found that an annual Faith Supper is very successful. Regular members are invited to bring a sweet or a savoury to make up a buffet, and to invite friends to join them for a social evening, perhaps with some presented by a good local Christian singer or band for twenty minutes or so. There may be a place for a brief epilogue, which introduces the Christian faith in a seeker-friendly way.

9. Some form of lively and good natured competition between groups, such as a quiz, or a board games evening has an occasional place in the total programme. It helps with social interaction.

10. A good Christian Video has an annual place in the programme. It needs to be pre-viewed - some are dated or rather crass. You must have good equipment and everyone must be able to see and hear.

It is of course very important for your group to remain permanently missionary in spirit, so that new members are always sought and warmly welcomed when they arrive. We eventually sought to set down ways in which we could encourage members to do this, and I include these here:

CONSIDERATION OF WAYS IN WHICH GROUP MEMBERS CAN INVITE AND WELCOME PEOPLE TO THE GROUP

1. **Talking to them about the Group**
    When inviting teenagers, refer to it in conversation as a Youth Group. With those in their twenties call it a Christian Group, You need to get to know them first. Be honest without being threatening. You might use an approval like the following:

    'We are a group of Christian in their teens and twenties, with a couple of older leaders, who meet on Monday nights at eight to consider various aspects of the Christian faith and modern day problems in a varied and informal way. The programme is different each week. We are open to anyone who is in that age range coming along, and we're hoping to grow too large for a house so that we find another informal, comfortable meeting place for larger numbers. Would you like to come next week, or in a week or two? I can meet you if you like."

    Be honest; be prepared to answer questions. Put your invitation in a way they can grasp. If you have to wait for an answer, ask them informally when talking together, without being heavy; pray before hand, and remember what they say or do may be different from what they're thinking. Give them time, and gently pursue your invitation unless they seriously warn you off.

2. **Welcoming them to the Group**

The basic rule is never let them feel embarrassed or uncomfortable if you can avoid it. Stick with them when they first come and introduce them informally to others. Only gradually loosen the ties as they gain confidence. Remember that older leaders only provide the basic framework of friendliness, conversation and hospitality; those you have invited need to get to know their peers. Do not pressurise them to speak or participate. Let them move at their own pace.

3. **Questions to ask when you meet a newcomer**

'My name's Fred. What's yours. Are you at Work? (Don't assume they are at school unless they are clearly 14,15 or 16). What do you do? If at school or college, what subjects are you studying?'

Try to get them to talk about their interest, perhaps by talking about one of yours first. Always look for points of common interest, and develop these. Humour is very useful. Tell a story against yourself if possible. BUT don't make fun of them! Then try to involve them in a conversation with a couple of others on a non religious topic. Some will be comfortable just to listen; you can tell by the faces of others that being silent is making them feel more shy, so they then need to revert to a conversation with just you. For the whole of the evening, and especially before and after the formal proceedings, keep your eyes open, and don't let newcomers or relative newcomers sit alone, while others are talking around them. This makes a person feel really uptight. Go over to them. Bring them in to a conversation. Remember that if you are shy, they are shyer. And don't worry if you struggle. They will appreciate your vulnerability; it makes them feel at home! Having said that, don't let an awesome silence grow between you. Just say; 'I've run out of things to say. Let's go and talk to .... Or, let's go and .... Or, can you help me with....' It's best not to do this across the sexes in any depth, if you are the same peer group. A short friendly conversation is O.K. But don't get heavy (unless you want to!)- it might be misinterpreted!

BE ENCOURAGED!

I hope these brief introductions to the developing life of a Christian youth group will prove useful. You will have observed that there is much to planning a programme. It does involve a heavy commitment involving time, talent and energies. Christian Youth work is as much a calling as any other form of ministry within the Church, and those who are so called should be prepared to give themselves to the task. Do not be overwhelmed by the thought of what you have to do; small beginnings are always best. If you take the handful of young people with whom you have contact, bring them together on a particular evening at a particular time, begin by planning a month's programme, follow carefully some of the ideas contained here and pray for them, you will be surprised how you begin to see come results. I wish you every blessing as you begin.

THE PROBLEMS

Any kind of leadership inevitably involves hassles and problems. If we want to remain in control of these, but under the control of the Spirit, we will avoid putting ourselves in a position where others use us as the focus for their own needs.

But if we pick up the baton of youth leadership, we must expect that we will be surrounded by an interesting variety of different demands which will come to us in waves day by day, week by week, certainly as long as we continue the youth group race, and even beyond the time when the baton is laid down. I thought it might be helpful to mention a few which seem to me to be fairly common and reasonably typical.

SOCIALISING

Many young people will want to use their youth group as a place for socialising alone. Their aim will be to make and build relationships in as attractive and entertaining a manner as possible. This is particularly difficult in the initial stages of building a youth group, when the youth leader is seeking to establish his aims and objectives. His members will be looking for social opportunities, rather than spiritual ones. You have to be very persistent and persuasive to win your members to a programme which looks at the other worldly in the light of this world. I was once told by a very wise Christian leader that if the least my youth group did was to enable its members to meet in a Christian context with a view to marriage and establishing Christian families, then I would have done a good work for the next generation, and it is certainly true that building harmonious and Christian homes is one very real objective of a Christian group, particularly in present society. But if that is all that the group does, then much of its purpose will have been missed.

It is absolutely great when the youth group has passed through a whole generation, and the children of those who were members start attending evening meetings themselves. Perhaps for the first time you will have parents who sympathise with and properly understand what the aims of your programme are, but you will only reach this stage if that programme has contained rather more than the opportunity to make relationships. So resist the demand for a purely social programme. Do not be satisfied with table tennis and billiards and outings. Be careful how often you plan a disco and what its content is. Look to providing constant Christian education. If your young people are awkward in response to this and some of them leave, then just take this as par for the course. When it becomes apparent that you are quietly but strongly determined to pursue a particular programme, then those who are interested in such a programme will make themselves known. Provided your advertising is good and the signals you give are right, then over a period of time, you will gradually build a core of those who seek what you provide, and around them others will gather, perhaps for socialising purposes initially, but then increasingly attracted to the powerful spiritual nature of your programme.

BEE IN THE BONNET

You will meet occasionally the 'bee in the bonnet' type, who will seek to use the group as a vehicle for his particular idea or ministry. He may want to press his ideas about abortion or hanging or animal rights or some other significant contemporary issue upon others, and may not be willing to discuss anything which moves outside the particular interest he has. This can be a nuisance in discussion groups, though strong leaders are able to divert or silence difficult members like this. He is much more difficult in social times such as the opening or closing of an evening's session, when he may buttonhole young and unsuspecting new members, and talk to them ceaselessly about his particular idea, sometimes even pressing leaflets or information packs upon them. You may have to pursue him round the room, or have a strong private word with him. It is sometimes necessary to ask such people to leave.

LEADERSHIP

Some young people have an inbuilt desire to be leaders, and this has to be nurtured and guided. An anti-establishment attitude is sometimes an expression of this. If you have a few caged lions roaring against you, investigate their leadership potential. Look particularly for a young person who has good judgement, a clear sign of leadership potential. If you can, give such a person an increasing degree of responsibility amongst her or his peers, and let her/him work with an older adult, so that she/he is steadily influenced by more mature leadership skills, as it may be that in the teenage years, some ideas that she/he has may be unbalanced and lacking spiritual wisdom. Does it go without saying that those who exercise leadership should first be committed Christians? It is hard work being a leader, and they need to cultivate a servant heart. Putting away the chairs, sweeping the room, and picking up the song books are jobs for leaders too! Meet anti-establishment criticism with sweet reason, and seek always to maintain an atmosphere of friendship and love. Try to separate the critical ideas which come your way from your personal relationships with those who make them, and try to deal with your own aggressions and frustrations outside that situation. A wise Christian friend can be useful as a punch-bag when you are under pressure. Don't allow the one issue critic to take a lead until he has become more balanced. Seek for those who, though quiet and inexperienced, may have hidden potential to lead others.

MISFITS

At the other end of the scale there will be those who find it difficult to fit in. Some will have social and communication problems: they will not necessarily want to take a leadership role, but they will often seek attention. Some of them feed on it, and will behave in many peculiar ways in order to achieve it. It is very hard to love the unlovely, but you will be required to exercise patience, tolerance and understanding, and sometimes to be firm when love demands it.

One of the hardest things to deal with is a group that is closed and not prepared to admit to its circle those whose faces do not fit. Like us all, young people can be cliquey, and may seek to exclude those who have never been part of their group of friends. You will need to encourage openness both by example and by direct teaching. Everyone who comes along to your group will need to be welcomed warmly, and helped to be part of all that is going on. I have found it helps to approach individual regular members with a request to go and speak to someone who has just arrived, and to introduce them to other members. Shyness and embarrassment might make conversation difficult, but elsewhere I have suggested lines of conversation which usually begin with discovering who a person is, and what he or she does. It is important also for the youth leader to make himself known briefly but in a friendly manner to those who have just arrived, and then to introduce them to someone else. Everyone can fit in if they are prepared to make an effort, but it is useful to point out to new members that they should not judge the group meeting on what they discover on the first night they attend. We all need to adjust to new experiences, and any attender would do well to come to three or four meetings before making up his mind about whether the group is suitable for him.

DRIVES

Most of the young people in your charge will have the normal drives of their age group of course. I'm not just thinking about the sex drive, though Christian teaching about sex, love and marriage is an obvious and constant regular in the group programme. Wanting to serve and help others is another such drive. Nothing could be more healthy or more implicitly Christian, but don't allow this drive to dominate so that humanist do-gooding becomes your sole purpose. Service of others needs to be sanctified by Christian love explicitly, and empowered by the Holy Spirit. It will naturally flow from conversion, and a number of conversions will produce an eventual demand for a project of some kind. Such a project which explicitly includes a declaration of its Christian source is to be preferred to one which makes no reference to Christ. Any money raising needs to be directed towards specific projects, results of which can be seen by members, whether they be international, national or local. Making sure that social concern has a proper and balanced place in your programme is an ongoing difficulty. It can over-dominate, or not have sufficient emphasis. Where it has its proper place, it teaches what it is to love others. And it is possible to discover God by loving others, though the leader needs to give the appropriate guidance and direction if this aim is to be realised.

ADULTS

Much of your work will meet problems which are caused by adults. Some adults suspect young people because their image does not conform to adult respectability; they fear their self-confidence; if the adults are churchgoers whose faith is in difficulties, then, sometimes, the generation gap that they imagine exists is just a spirituality gap, particularly after some members of your group have discovered real Christian faith. Some young people on their side do not like or appreciate the life style of the older generation, think that they know things from which older people are excluded, and have to be encouraged into church going, which can seem or be boring, irrelevant and out of date; they often need to be educated into the reason for the Church's existence and mission. To bring the adult and adolescent generations together is a constant battle.

Whatever the problem is, grasp the nettle; don't run away; be firm and loving and know where you stand. You will find much joy in resolving problems, and through their resolution your group will grow and develop.

THE PURPOSE

Jesus instructed His disciples to set their minds on God's Kingdom and His righteousness. This was to be their first priority. And this was what produced successful fruit in terms of the growth of God's Kingdom. He knew this to be true in his own ministry. After His baptism, which was the moment which marked His acceptance of God's purpose for Him, He went into the wilderness of Judea to face the test of Satan, a test which would determine whether or not God's priorities were his own. Here he struggled to sort out priorities in the establishment of the Kingdom of God. When He considered His own physical hunger after forty days, and the abject hunger and poverty of His people, He knew God had given Him the power to turn even stones into bread, and that He could use that power to meet all their worldly needs. This would have been good, but it would not have been the best He could do. This was a subtle temptation of Satan, for to do good rather than the best was to be diverted from the real task at hand. 'Man is not to live on bread alone, but on every word that comes from the mouth of God'. True life is brought by the word of God, and true life is not just eating and drinking, but it is spiritual bread, the bread of eternal life. For when all men's physical needs are satisfied, there is still an inner hunger, a deep longing for reality and purpose, an often unconscious desire to know God. This hunger was what Jesus was first and foremost required by His Father to satisfy, and although his ministry would never be solely this, it would be with the pointed spear of spiritual penetration that his attack on men's souls would be made.

Then Jesus found himself looking down from the dizzy heights of the pinnacle of the Temple gate on to the enquiring, seeking eyes of the crowds who gathered there; perhaps His mind's eye reported to His brain that the enemy was telling him that a miraculous demonstration of power would produce an immediate response from those He hoped to convert - immediate, but not long lasting. A dazzling and glamorous display of power, a Houdini like box of tricks, would test the truth of what He had come to believe, and if He were gathered up by God's angels as He threw himself into the air, there would be proof for His watchers where they had previously only had faith. But again He answered the temptation by Scripture; 'You are not to put the Lord your God to the Test'. His Father did not intend that faith was to be turned into an explosion of proof; it was to begin in the minds of men like a mustard seed, small, frail and hidden in the hearts of seekers after the Kingdom.

Nor was the Kingdom to be established by force. The conquest of the Romans or of any other occupying power was what every Jew dreamed about, and to lead the armies producing such victory would be to assume the sort of leadership role which all men would envy. This was the third temptation. Yet to impose such a Kingdom of conquest of men's unwilling minds was again a tactic of Satan; and to do it by paying homage to the destroyer of men's souls was impossible for the one who brought salvation: 'Scripture says, 'You shall do homage to the Lord your God and worship Him alone'. He knew that the Kingdom only had reality when it was accepted willingly and gladly by those whose souls were freely conquered by its irresistible magic.

So Christ's priority became, probably always was, the establishment of the Kingdom, that spiritual Kingdom entered into by all those who made God King when they discovered Him through the life and ministry of his Son - and any other way of establishing that Kingdom would serve only the devices of the enemy, and would ultimately lead to disaster. Christ knew he must respond to the call of the Father made at His baptism to serve mankind, and suffer through that service so that all men may have the opportunity to follow the way of the cross.

His message to mankind was well reported by Mark at the beginning of his gospel; 'The time has arrived; the Kingdom of God is upon you; repent, and believe the Gospel'. His first priority was to enable men to turn to God, and accept His kingly rule over their lives. His life of love and example, His teaching, preaching and healing, were in themselves a valuable contribution to men's understanding of God and each added to the working out of His first priority. When men asked him to perform more miracles, Jesus told his disciples they must move on to other villages to preach the gospel, for that was the reason why He had come. When at Caesarea Philippi, Peter ruined His recognition of Jesus' Messiahship by trying to discourage him from the path of service and suffering, Mark's Gospel tells us that Jesus was led to talk about the reality of losing self for the sake of the gospel. And when He strode purposefully on towards Jerusalem, His disciples were amazed that he dared to face, in the name of the Kingdom, the end that awaited him there.

Jesus preached the Gospel of first priority; He lived the life of first priority. He knew that what mattered most was to see men's lives against the background of eternity. Sometimes I think that some churches have lost this gospel of first priority, or confuse the order of priority, or make the mistake of treating all Christian priorities equally. When they do so, they lose all power and relevance, because they are no longer true to Jesus Christ.

Youth work, like all other forms of Christian work, must reflect this gospel of first priority. If youth leaders are to be ministers of Christ to young people, their ministry must reflect His. Just as He first cared for men's eternal souls, and their here and now response to God's Kingly rule, so they must place the eternal souls of those placed in their care before every other need they have. Other needs must not be neglected. They are to be met and coped with, but only within the context that all men are made in the image of God, and are created to praise and glorify Him for ever.

'So Jesus went all around the towns and villages teaching in their synagogues, proclaiming the good news of the Kingdom and curing every kind of illness and infirmity'. (Matthew 9 v.35) Teaching, preaching, healing - the three fold ministry of Jesus, a ministry which was effective during His lifetime, and effective again in the Holy Spirit empowered ministry of the early Church. Though Jesus performed many remarkable miracles, much of His work must have been patient and unspectacular, dogged by failures and disappointments, and increasingly pressurised as the last days drew near. It would have been possible to be diverted from His central aim, to swerve away from the clear path ahead. Yet his single mindedness was unswerving - the straight bold shadow of the Cross led Him forward along the narrow path which led to the salvation of mankind. And He had the grace and courage and personality to follow that path whatever the consequences, for although truly human, He was also the incarnate God.

So He set out for us our calling. It is a lesson I keep on learning afresh, even though I instinctively started out on it when I was first a youth leader. For many of those considering working with young people it is easy to hear the siren voices which say 'Young people aren't interested in spiritual matters these days. They find such things boring, outdated and irrelevant. If you want to be effective, you must concentrate on the social or moral, or offer them the life style of the world within the context of the faith.' Is that so? - I think not. What a youth leader needs as much as anything else is the ability to plough the straight furrow patiently and persistently, following the pattern of the Master. Then with prayer and the power of the Spirit, he will find significant and lasting results over the years, and though there will be opposition and difficulty, he will begin to change his community and the individuals within it, to produce the renewal and revival all Christians seek.

A. Teaching

Gather together a group of people of any age and of mixed Church and non Church background, and ask them to complete a questionnaire on their knowledge of the Christian faith, with some such questions as these in it: What is the Incarnation? Was Jesus the Son of God? Did the resurrection really happen? How are we saved from sin? What is the body of Christ? and so on. You will quickly confirm that many British people know little of things biblical and theological. In fact many of the questions you ask will never have been considered before by a large proportion of your random sample. Many of the terms you use they will never have heard before. They are children of a 'post Christian' era. In the U.K. many people no longer talk of spiritual matters; discussion of religion is unfashionable in many quarters and embarrassing to many, though there are signs that this is gradually changing. Those who have faith are 'encouraged' to keep it to themselves. The names of God and Jesus are used liberally in pubs and clubs, on T.V. and the cinema screen, but knowledge of Christian claims about them is often limited to the infantile days of primary school. Religious education in the teenage years is often inadequate because many of those who give it don't believe it or understand it. The majority do not attend Church or Sunday School regularly.

So, for the majority, their understanding of religious concepts has not grown alongside their thinking in other areas. It is therefore their own infantile thoughts about God that they often reject. Ah, you say, but the questions you would have me ask in this questionnaire are the sort that only a theologian can be expected to answer. Are they really? Read some of the material used by the Church and by a much wider band of people even as recently as the end of the nineteenth century, and see how ordinary people were taught solid theology so that they understood the basics of Christian faith, even if they did not always make that faith personal to themselves. And in any case, if you were to ask that same group another set of simpler, purely biblical, questions, you may be alarmed to discover how little many of them know about religion at all. It is noticeable how often participants in T.V. games stumble over religious questions of considerable simplicity, whilst at the same time revealing the depth of their knowledge and understanding in many other areas. What are the names of the four gospels? What are the Beatitudes? Who was converted on the Damascus road? Name six of the twelve disciples. The answers are often funny, were they not for the Christian rather frightening. You see, we do live in a post Christian missionary situation in this country, and there is a great need for plain and simple teaching.

Although strenuous attempts are continuously being made to improve the quality of Religious Education in schools, and though the Education Reform Act insists on a broadly Christian syllabus, much ground has been lost since 1944. Knowledge of the plain facts of the Bible and the theology of the Christian faith has declined alongside the increased emphasis in many state schools on learning about other religions, recognition of religious consciousness, and the desire to inculcate 'correct' moral attitudes. There has been a wholesale, widespread decline in the Sunday School movement, both in the number of scholars attending, and, in many places, the quality of teaching. This has been partly compensated for by the growth of Church based organisations like Crusaders and Covenantors, but generally today most young people remain outside Church based organisations of any kind, and belong firmly to the unchurched.

There is therefore a primary need to communicate the elements of the Christian faith to the young simply and effectively. It is always better if understanding precedes Christian commitment, as that understanding forms a base upon which religious experience may stand, and from which answers to the complex problems of life may be drawn.

Jesus called disciples, and the word 'disciples' means a learner. These men were learners in the school of Christ, and His plain but deep teaching, for example in the Sermon on the Mount, and the teaching example of His life itself, led them eventually to place their trust in him as Lord and Saviour. If youth leaders are to lead young men and women to their Saviour, they must come to understand His claims. That is the basic reason for a carefully organised teaching programme as the backbone of all youth work.

B. Preaching

Preaching is essentially proclamation, the 'kerygma' of the early church. Just as the herald, the 'kerux' proclaims the coming of the King, so the Christian proclaims the coming of Jesus. And the pattern of the 'kerygma' in the Acts of the Apostles reminds us of the effectiveness of reciting the plain facts of the Christian faith; here was a man named Jesus who went about doing good, who was arrested and tried by wicked men, who died on a cross, and rose again from the dead; He will come again, and He calls men everywhere to repentance. 'What shall we do about it?' the people cried to Peter at the end of his first sermon. So they were plainly told that they should repent and be baptised and turn to Christ in faith. The plain preaching of Acts during that period in history, when the Church grew as it has never grown since, reminds us of what preaching really is. Preaching convicts men's hearts, and demands response. It convicts because it is given under the direction and inspiration of the Holy Spirit, and it demands response because it is that same Holy Spirit who is causing spiritual activity in the minds and hearts of those who listen. Sometimes modern preaching is not real preaching; it is just a few thoughts, and ideas of a man, a collection of pious phrases, an intellectual wrestle, a hurried assembly of topical points. But real preaching is directed by God, it comes from a life of prayer and closeness to God, and it is a message given through a person to those he does not know, but the Father knows. It often calls to conversion or commitment; it often points to growth and holiness. It always exalts the Lord and his Kingdom. And it is inextricably intertwined with teaching, for the one feeds the other. Everyone needs to hear the Gospel plainly expounded. If those in their teens and twenties are never given the opportunity to respond to its reality in the manner of the disciple Thomas, then it is no wonder that they leave the 'club' to which they never really belonged before the years of parenting set in. Any programme designed for young people must give them the opportunity to respond in any one of a thousand ways to the thrilling challenge of Jesus Christ. So many good youth leaders do everything but this; somehow they think that to be evangelical is to be embarrassing, or to be straightforwardly spiritual is to put young people off. And yet it is normal, it is plain human, to want to find the purpose and plan of our lives. The young seek this, and we sell them short if, by the sin of omission, we allow them to drift into cults and isms, or into the nemesis of worldliness. The gospel of Jesus is a challenge to cross bearing, or is it nothing. And the young need to hear it!

C. Healing

This world is ruled by the Prince of Darkness. The Bible explicitly teaches that Satan has made the earth His Kingdom, and that the Paradise which God originally created has been marred, spoiled, by the activities of the powers of evil. This disruption shows itself in the presence of disease and suffering, unbelief, immorality, confusion, emotional and mental disturbances, the constant disruption of ordered society and so on. And we are born into the Kingdom of Satan without our choice; we are all infected, and the sin within us comes from what we inherit, what Satan encourages us into, and what we deliberately choose. We were made in the image of God, as was the world, but that image is spoiled by our conscious or unconscious acceptance of the membership of Satan's Kingdom. We have therefore two choices: we can remain where we are, or we can choose to leave that Kingdom and join the Kingdom of God, obey the rule of God and live for Christ.

And as Jesus establishes His Kingdom in the lives of men, so He brings healing of body, mind and soul. The promise is that His Kingdom will eventually be established on earth, as well as in heaven, and His disciples are called to advance that Kingdom step by step. So 'healing' is not just about healing of the body, though it certainly includes that. Jesus the Sovereign Messiah had the power to rid men's bodies of disease, to take away leprosy, blindness, deafness, to straighten twisted limbs, and even to break the barrier of death itself. The Church today is turning itself to this third part of the ministry of Jesus, and is rediscovering the power of the Holy Spirit to continue the ministry He began, so that healing services are taking place, and the laying on of hands practised, often with results which demonstrate the power of the Kingdom of God to drive back that other Kingdom effectively and speedily. But healing also includes the healing in mind and spirit, the reconciliation of relationships, and the mending of the use of time, talents and possessions.

Many young people, like those of every age, are bound by the effects of the Kingdom of Satan on their lives. The need the law of love to dominate them so that they can make meaningful relationships with their peers, their parents, their workmates, their boyfriends or girlfriends. They need the mending of diseased attitudes to sex, of bored and purposeless searching for meaning, of lostness and loneliness and lack of identity. They need to be made whole, to be made complete people, to stand mature in Christ.

Jesus saw the close connections between the diseases of mind, body and of spirit. When he raised the paralysed man, He forgave him his sins first, for He knew that the disease of unforgiven sin caused, in this particular case, the disease of the body. And many of our hospital beds are filled with those broken in mind and spirit, whose brokenness is destroying their bodies. The youth leader can play his part in bringing the healing of Jesus into the midst of such brokenness wherever it is found.

BE FILLED WITH THE SPIRIT

To be involved in any kind of youth work is to be caught up in an infinitely complex, time consuming and exhausting activity. But Christian youth work is the most demanding of all, for it demands a ministry from the leader which can be patterned on the ministry of Christ. The servant leader is called to exercise that same ministry of teaching, preaching and healing among twentieth century young people. And he needs the same life of prayer, obedience and sacrifice as His Master; this is the way to a continuing, effective, ministry. The Christian youth leader must therefore be a Christian himself or herself, almost a truism were it not that many sincere dabblers have no living faith relationship of their own, and so have nothing to pass on. But more than that, the Christian youth leader must be Spirit filled, because he or she could not do the work in his or her own strength; he or she needs the constant support, encouragement and stimulation of the living Jesus within.

EPILOGUE

At the end of discussion group time almost every Sunday evening for twenty four years I called, 'Two minutes please!' to give each group the chance to wind up its evening deliberations, and this became a catch phrase of several generations of teens and twenties who have passed through the Methodist youth group I have led. I've spent hours each week in preparation, and hundreds of evenings in delivery. And almost every Sunday evening I've given out the notices, checked on the coffee arrangements, supervised the pattern of the evening, and at ten thirty or so switched out the lights and locked all the doors. These mundane aspects of being a Christian youth leader have been compensated for by meeting and knowing as friends some wonderful people; many of them have discovered the Christian faith for the first time as a direct result of the activities of the youth group, and are continuing to serve the Lord around the country, and some in the wider world; some of them have been wonderfully supportive as leaders in 'the Group', as it has long been affectionately known. I would like to thank them all - the talented, the strange, the awkward, the antagonistic, the supportive, the lively and the sociable. I've learned from them all, and it is on their experience, as well as my own, that I have drawn in writing this book. It has seemed to me for some time that some of this experience should be shared. In a decade when there are great signs of hope in certain sections of the Church in this country, and when the young are increasingly ready to listen to the voice of the gospel, it is the direct spiritual approach which I believe all youth group leaders should adopt, and what you have read in the last four chapters is intended to be the programme for such an approach. In a continuing busy life, it is good to take time and reflect on those aspects of the work which have produced results, and offer them to a wider audience. So I hope all these ideas prove to be as effective for the Kingdom in your Nazareth as they have proved to be in mine.